Fearless Words

Fearless Words

How to Write Impactful Copy for Authentic Influence and Sales

Georgina L. Nestor

authors AND CO.

First published in Great Britain in 2024
by Authors & Co.
www.authorsandco.pub

Copyright © Georgina L. Nestor 2024

Georgina L. Nestor asserts the moral right to be identified as the author of this work in accordance with the Copyright, Designs and Patents Act 1988.

ISBN 978-1-915771-84-1 (paperback)

All rights reserved. No part of this book may be reproduced or transmitted in any form or by any means, electronic or mechanical, including photocopying, recording, or by any information storage and retrieval system without the written permission of the author, except where permitted by law or for the use of brief quotations in a book review.

This book is dedicated to the silent voices and the unseen visions. To those who hold a universe of ideas within, yet feel invisible in a world clamouring for attention. It is for the dreamers who've ever felt their message lost in the void, and for the creators whose brilliance remains cloaked in shadows of doubt.

If you dare to feel the fear and step forward anyway, your courage lights a path for others in the dark.

And if you feel the fear and choose to stay hidden for now, please know that your voice matters, your message is important, and the world is waiting for you to find your moment of bravery.

This book is for all who believe their stories are too small, their voices too quiet or their ideas too unconventional. Here is to finding the strength to share your unique light with the world, in your own time and in your own way.

Every journey begins with a single step. May you find in these pages the courage to take yours, and to become just a little more fearless in expressing your truth.

Contents

Introduction

The difference between being the world's best-kept secret and becoming the name on everyone's lips lies in the power, clarity and authenticity of your voice. Excelling in your field counts for little if you remain unseen – this stark reality confronts countless business owners who, despite their expertise and unparalleled skills, remain shadows in their industries.

Just imagine creating a masterpiece, only to tuck it away in a dark room where no eyes can appreciate its beauty. In the vast, interconnected world of today – especially the digital expanse that connects continents in milliseconds – your talent alone isn't enough to guarantee recognition or success.

In an era where attention has become the ultimate currency, yet is more fleeting than ever before, the brilliance of your work, the depth of your knowledge or the uniqueness of your services doesn't automatically translate to visibility, acclaim or cash in the bank. In this relentless quest for recognition, the journey of overcoming personal barriers to find and use one's voice becomes not just relevant, but essential.

Why this book matters

Picture moving from a place of doubt and hesitation to shining brightly through expressive impact in your business. This book paves the way for such a transformation – yours, specifically. Alongside, I'll share the adversities I've faced to illuminate your path towards mastering your unique voice with both confidence and clarity.

My own journey, defined by years under the shadow of bullying and trauma, unveiled the true potency of voice. It is far more than just a vehicle for being heard; it is a catalyst for change, a stand against injustice and a way to challenge ridicule. Today, my voice serves as both protection and illumination, not as a marker of personal victory, but as proof of what you can achieve when you defy the constraints of fear.

Designed to arm you with effective strategies and insights, this book is going to encourage you to step up boldly, leverage your voice to distinguish yourself and forge meaningful impacts. It is an invitation to shape your unique experiences and viewpoints into stories that not only engage, but inspire action and create genuine connections.

As we navigate this journey together, remember, your voice is a powerful instrument of change. It is not just about speaking louder – depth always holds more power than decibels - it is about speaking truer. By the end of this book, my hope is that you'll not only find your voice but, master the art of using it with purpose – transforming not just your business, but the lives of those you reach.

Beyond skill and talent: being the voice that resonates

The world of online business is more crowded than ever, full of voices battling for a moment in the spotlight. Here, even the most skilled and knowledgeable among us can find ourselves lost in the noise, our potential impact muffled by the sheer volume of competition.

But what truly distinguishes those who break through from those who fade into obscurity isn't just relentless effort or raw talent - nor is it merely having solid business skills or the constant pursuit of excellence. These are important, yes, but they're not the deciding factor.

The key differentiator - the bridge between anonymity and recognition, obscurity and eminence - is how effectively you find and project your unique voice. Your voice is more than the words you speak or write; it is the embodiment of your values, your vision and your approach to your craft. It is how you communicate not just what you do, but who you are and why it matters.

And in the clamour of the online business world, where everyone has a platform and everyone is constantly broadcasting, your voice is your superpower. It makes you resonate with your audience, cut through the noise and not just be seen, but be remembered and sought after.

Talent, while essential, forms just the foundation of your potential. Tenacity, business know-how and the continuous honing of your skills are the building blocks of success. Yet, without a voice that carries your message, your story and your unique proposition to the right ears, even the most formidable expertise runs the risk of remaining the world's best-kept secret.

Unlocking your unique voice: the path to transformative communication

As we peel back the layers of what makes a voice not just heard, but followed, we venture into the heart of this book's promise: actionable insights and real-world strategies that transform communication.

First, we'll dissect the essence of a personal brand and look into the significance of your voice in today's digital deluge. You will discover not just the importance of your voice, but how to unearth and refine it, turning away from the paralysing quest for perfection, instead aiming for authentic expression.

Then, the focus shifts from theory to tangible action. From the basics of crafting compelling communication to fine-tuning your brand's voice, we explore the nuances of tone, the distinction between your written and spoken voice, and the pitfalls that could mute your message. You will apply what you learn directly to your business, ensuring that your voice doesn't end up echoing in the void, but instead reaches and resonates with your intended audience.

One of the greatest myths I aim to dismantle as you journey through this book is the notion that impactful writing is the exclusive domain of 'natural' writers. I am challenging that misconception head-on, offering a testament to the power of learned skill and honed voice over what many would describe as innate talent.

So whether you're at the cusp of starting your business journey or seeking to elevate an existing venture, the essence of this book is to show that your voice, once uncovered and unleashed, is your most potent tool.

The courage to be fearless

Now, this is where fearlessness comes into play - that's the key to *truly* using your voice.

And to be clear, fearlessness isn't about recklessness; it is about courageously sharing your ideas, even when the stakes are high and the audience seems vast and unknown. It is about daring to be heard, standing for what you believe in and presenting your vision to the world without flinching.

This boldness is what transforms a whisper into a rally cry and a message into a movement. With fearlessness, your voice becomes not just audible, but influential. This book is going to be your cheerleader and guide rolled into one. It is your ticket to not just success, but a legacy that lasts.

Together, we're going to dive into how to uncover your voice and use it to pull the right people in, make them listen and entice them to buy. After all, your business can help people, right? Maybe it even changes lives.

So think of it like this: being seen is the first hurdle. It is about capturing attention in a landscape saturated with messages and distractions. But visibility alone isn't enough. Once you've caught the eye, the next challenge is to be truly listened to. In our fast-paced, information-overloaded environment, earning someone's time to listen – to really hear and understand your message – is invaluable.

And the final, most crucial step is to be believed. It is one thing for your audience to know of you and like what you present, but trust is deeper; it is about belief in your integrity, your values and your promises.

Evolving beyond 'know, like and trust'

The traditional marketing framework of 'know, like and trust' lays the groundwork, but in today's digital age, these concepts have evolved. Now more than ever, authenticity and a genuine brand identity are what propel you from mere recognition to real connection.

Why? Because authenticity cuts through noise, and in a world teeming with curated personas and polished veneers, genuine voices stand out. Authenticity brings about a deeper level of engagement; it transforms passive observers into active participants who feel a personal stake in your journey and your success.

A real brand identity, one that's carefully crafted and true to your values, not only helps you stand out, but builds a community. It resonates on a personal level, touching on shared experiences, dreams and challenges. This resonance is what transforms 'know, like and trust' from a marketing mantra into a lived experience for your audience.

It is what makes being seen, listened to and believed not just marketing goals, but milestones of genuine connection.

So as we move forward, remember, the path to making a real difference with your business lies not just in being known, liked and trusted; it is in being authentic, creating a brand identity that's unmistakably yours and building connections that go beyond transactions to touch lives deeply.

Are you ready to really turn up the volume on your voice? To not just take up space, but to own it unapologetically? Your voice isn't merely a route to success; it is the essence of your uniqueness, the heart of your business and the fuel for all your dreams. Beyond that, it's the catalyst for that change you can bring about in your clients' lives.

Shall we begin?

1
The Genesis of Fear

Every journey of influence begins not just with a word, but with a choice: the decision to speak despite the fear. In this chapter, I'm taking you deep into the heart of fear, uncovering its unexpected strength, and learning how to use this potent emotion to its advantage, to fuel our communication.

For me, fear has been a lifelong companion. My memories as a teenager are coloured by instances of severe bullying, each word and act of aggression embedding itself into my psyche, shaping my interactions and my self-perception. The echoes of the school bus filled with the sounds of ridicule and several instances of physical violence followed me long after the days turned into years. The loss of a close friend to suicide at sixteen - a pivotal moment that could have been about growth and discovery when navigating sudden and severe grief - became about loss, vulnerability and the fear of being abandoned. Adulthood didn't spell the end of such experiences; bullying and abuse found its way through various new doors, reinforcing the old voices that whispered I was never enough.

Why share this with you? Because it is through this lens of personal adversity that the concept of fearlessness in communication, especially in business, becomes most poignant. Fear, I've discovered, doesn't preclude us from having a voice; rather, it offers a profound reason to find and use it.

Fearlessness is not the absence of fear

The word 'fearless' often conjures images of superheroes and stoic warriors, figures unblemished by doubt. Yet, the reality is starkly different. Being fearless isn't about the absence of fear; it is about feeling that churn in your stomach, that tightening in your chest, and stepping forward anyway. It is about using that fear as a catalyst rather than a cage.

In business and writing, the fear of judgement can be paralysing. The digital world, with its immediate feedback loops and pervasive reach, often amplifies this fear. The thought of pressing 'publish' on a social media post or sending out a newsletter can feel like standing at the edge of a cliff. What if you are misunderstood? What if your words invite criticism, or worse, indifference?

But here's the twist: being judged is inevitable. The mere act of existence, of having opinions, tastes and preferences, opens us up to judgement. You prefer tea over coffee, cats over dogs - such simple preferences can divide opinions. Recognising this inevitability is the first step towards embracing fearlessness. If judgement is a given, the fear of it need not be a barrier.

How, then, do we turn fear from a silencer into a megaphone? The answer lies in authenticity and the raw, unfiltered expression of our true selves. Authentic communication resonates *because* it is real. It connects on a human level, cutting through the noise of polished sales pitches and curated feeds. When you share your story, your expertise and your ideas imbued with your personal truth, your words gain the power to not just reach but touch and transform others.

Consider the idea that the very fears that you feel are likely shared by many of your readers and potential clients. By voicing these fears, you not only liberate yourself from their hold but offer solace to others. Your courage in sharing becomes a beacon for those still struggling in silence.

Crafting fearless words

In the subsequent chapters, we will explore how to find and use words that are not just heard but felt. We will explore strategies for developing a voice that is both bold and vulnerable, authoritative yet approachable. From the structure of your sentences to the choice of your stories, every element of your writing can embody the spirit of fearlessness. We will look at practical examples, dissecting pieces of writing that have successfully turned fear into a catalyst for change and growth.

More than just techniques, however, this chapter is an invitation - an invitation to journey through your fears and emerge not unscathed but undefeated, to recognise that every word you write, every message you craft, is an act of bravery, and to understand that in the world of communication, the most impactful words are those spoken from a place of deep truth and vulnerability.

As we proceed, please remember that your voice is unique. It is shaped by your experiences, your values and your dreams. No one else in the universe has those. It is tempered by your battles, both won and lost. This voice can be your greatest asset in the crowded marketplace of ideas. When used effectively, it has the power to not only capture attention, but to inspire action, create and deepen connections, and catalyse real, lasting change.

Embracing fearlessness in your writing doesn't require you to change who you are; it invites you to simply *be* who you are, completely and unapologetically. I mean, why would you ever apologise for who you are anyway? It challenges you to speak even when your voice shakes, to share even when the stakes are high, and to believe that in a world of noise, your voice matters perhaps more than you've ever dared to imagine.

By the end of this book, I hope you will not only understand the power of fearless writing, but feel equipped to begin practising it. In your hands lies the ability to mould perceptions, shift narratives and influence outcomes. With each fearless word, you are not just communicating; you are transforming yourself, your business and the world around you.

As we close this chapter on embracing fear and really finding and owning your fearless voice, we are well prepared to take the next step in our journey of influence. The courage to be who we are, unapologetically and authentically, sets the stage for how we present ourselves to the world.

This is not just about being heard; it is about being recognised and remembered. It leads us directly into the heart of personal branding, a concept that has become not just beneficial but essential for anyone looking to make a mark in today's digital landscape. In the next chapter, we will explore how personal branding extends the power of your voice, turning your unique experiences and values into a distinct, compelling brand that resonates deeply with your audience.

2
The Power of Personal Branding

In an age where individuality is more vital than ever before for small business owners like you and me, personal branding emerges not just as a strategy but as a necessity. Personal branding is the art of consistently presenting oneself and one's career as a complete brand. It is an amalgamation of skills, experiences and personality that you want the world to see you as. It is about carving a niche in the digital expanse, a space where your voice is not just heard but instantly recognised and valued.

This concept has evolved significantly with the advent of the digital age, transforming from a buzzword into a fundamental aspect of professional life. The digital age has democratised branding, shifting the focus from massive corporations to individuals, from broad to niche markets. Now, a well-crafted tweet, a poignant blog post or a compelling Instagram story can resonate as loudly, if not more so, than traditional advertising. The evolution of personal branding in today's world is characterised by this shift towards individuality and authenticity, making it possible for absolutely anyone to become a thought leader or an influencer in their domain.

Contrasting this with corporate branding reveals stark differences. Where corporate branding aims to communicate the values, mission and services of a business as a collective entity, personal branding is intrinsically linked to the *individual* behind the brand. It is personal branding that adds a human touch to the otherwise faceless entity of a corporation. It is about the creative who blogs about their failures and lessons, the stay-at-home mum with a side hustle who shares her creative process on social media, or the entrepreneur whose personal journey inspires their business ethos.

This individual-centric approach does more than just sell a product or a service; it builds a relationship. Personal branding, therefore, is not about boasting or self-promotion. Far from it, in fact. It is about storytelling, authenticity and connection. It is about making a promise to your audience about the unique value you bring, not just through what you do, but through who you are.

However, an intriguing aspect of personal branding lies in the perception it creates. While you may steer the ship of your brand with your values, stories and personality, it's ultimately the audience who decides what your personal brand stands for. This real connection can be both liberating and daunting. It underscores the importance of genuine engagement and consistent presentation of oneself, yet it also highlights that control is somewhat shared. Your audience's perceptions, their interactions with your brand and the meanings they derive from it play a significant role in shaping its identity.

Yet, this doesn't mean you're at the mercy of public opinion. There are, thankfully, effective strategies to ensure your personal brand is perceived in the light you intend. Consistency in your messaging, authenticity in your storytelling and regular engagement with your audience are key elements. By providing a clear, consistent and authentic narrative, you guide your audience's perception, nudging it towards the brand identity you aim to establish. This strategy helps not only in maintaining control over your personal brand's narrative, but in building deeper connections with your audience, more trust and, eventually, influencing how they see you in the digital marketplace.

In the digital marketplace, where everyone has access to the same tools and platforms, personal branding becomes the distinguishing factor. It is what sets you apart, making your voice not only distinct but deeply resonant in a sea of constant noise. So as we take a deeper look into the essence and significance of personal branding, we'll explore how mastering this art form is critical for anyone looking to influence, inspire and sell in today's world.

The importance of personal branding in the digital market

In today's digital marketplace, a cacophony of voices vies for attention. Social media feeds are inundated with content, emails flood inboxes, and advertisements pop up with every click. Standing out in this crowded space is not just challenging; it is akin to finding a needle in a digital haystack. This is where the power of personal branding becomes not just valuable, but absolutely vital.

Personal branding allows you to carve out an identity amidst the chaos, helping your audience find and connect with you in a truly meaningful way. By crafting a narrative that is distinctly yours, you transcend the generic and become memorable. Your stories, values and experiences become the colours with which you paint your digital persona, one that stands out for its authenticity and relatability.

But personal branding goes beyond just being noticed; it is about being remembered and, perhaps most importantly, trusted. Trust is the currency of the digital age – something that's hard-earned and very easily lost. In a world where scepticism towards faceless corporations is growing, personal brands offer that much-needed touchstone of authenticity. People are more likely to engage with and purchase from someone they feel they know and trust. Your personal brand becomes a testament to your authenticity, a way to demonstrate not only what you stand for but the integrity behind your words and actions.

This trust is cultivated over time through consistent, authentic engagement. It is about showing up as your true self, so-called 'flaws' and all, and sharing your journey with honesty. Personal branding allows you to build a community of followers, clients and collaborators who don't just buy what you're selling but really believe in your vision. They become advocates for your brand, driven by a genuine connection that goes well beyond the transaction.

The importance of personal branding in today's market, especially for small business owners, cannot be overstated. It is the linchpin of digital success and the secret that makes the difference between obscurity and renown. By establishing a strong personal brand, you not only navigate the digital marketplace more effectively, but you create a legacy that resonates with your core values and mission.

As we move forward, remember that personal branding is not a 'one and done' task but a continuous journey of self-discovery and communication. It is about aligning who you are with how you want to be seen and leveraging that authenticity to make a lasting impact in the digital world.

Personal branding and its impact on copywriting

A well-defined personal brand does more than just carve out a place for you in the digital world; it fundamentally transforms the way you communicate. Every piece of copy you create becomes a reflection of your personal brand, influencing its tone, style and content. This alignment ensures that your message not only reaches your audience but resonates with them on a personal level.

Before taking a deeper look at how personal branding transforms every aspect of your communication, let's pause to clarify what we mean by 'copy'. In the context of marketing and business, copy refers to the written content aimed at promoting a product, service or brand. This includes everything from website text, social media posts and email newsletters to blog articles, advertising scripts and press releases. Copy is a crucial tool for persuasion and engagement, designed to not only inform and entertain but elicit a response or action from the reader.

Great copy seamlessly blends promotional goals with storytelling, weaving your personal or brand identity into a narrative that resonates with your audience. It is the bridge between your brand's intentions and the audience's needs, carefully curated to convey your unique value proposition in a way that is both compelling and memorable. As we explore personal branding, understanding how to master your copy will be essential. It is not just about what you say, but how you say it that can turn interest into action and connections into conversions.

The tone of your copy becomes the voice of your personal brand, conveying your personality and values with each word. Whether you're nurturing a professional, authoritative voice or a playful, approachable one, your tone sets the stage for how your audience perceives and interacts with you. The style follows suit, encapsulating your unique approach to presentation and structure, which can range from formal and detailed to casual and concise. When it comes to content, a well-defined personal brand guides the topics you cover, ensuring they align with your brand's mission and resonate with your target audience's interests and needs.

Personal branding in the real world

Consider the towering presence of global fashion brands like Versace and H&M. Versace, with its luxurious allure and bold designs, stands as an epitome of fashion sophistication and Italian elegance. The brand resonates with a sense of exclusivity and high fashion, echoing the visionary spirit of its founder, Gianni Versace. Each piece, campaign and message from Versace imbues this signature style, appealing to those who seek the pinnacle of fashion and design.

In contrast, H&M, known for its accessibility and trendy yet affordable fashion, champions the democratisation of style. The brand's voice is approachable, inclusive and fashion-forward, crafting a narrative that appeals to a broad audience looking for the latest trends without the luxury price tag. Through collaborations with designers and celebrities, H&M bridges the gap between high fashion and the everyday consumer, proving that style doesn't have to come with a high cost.

Both Versace and H&M showcase the power of branding in shaping perception and consumer behaviour within the fashion industry. While Versace draws in those who yearn for luxury and exclusivity, H&M appeals to the desire for trendy, accessible fashion. Each brand leverages its unique identity to connect with its audience, illustrating that the essence of successful branding - whether in high fashion or fast fashion - lies in the consistent, authentic expression of core values and identity.

This principle of branding, grounded in authenticity and distinctiveness, is not confined to the realms of fashion; it is equally visible in the digital landscape we navigate daily.

As you scroll through your social media feed, personal branding emerges in the mosaic of posts from your favourite business owners and influencers. It is in the distinctive voice that makes a post unmistakably theirs, even before you see the name attached. Personal branding is the thread that weaves through their content, making each piece a reflection of their unique identity.

Notice how each influencer or business owner you like has a certain way of engaging with their audience that feels authentic to who they are. Maybe it's the entrepreneur who shares behind-the-scenes glimpses into their daily life, connecting personal experiences with professional insights. Or perhaps it's the influencer whose content is always infused with their signature humour or aesthetic, making their posts instantly recognisable amidst the endless scroll.

These personal touches are no accident – in fact, quite the opposite is true! They are carefully crafted aspects of personal branding, designed to create a connection that feels both personal and profound. This branding goes beyond mere aesthetics; it is about consistently communicating a core set of values, perspectives and stories that resonate with their audience. It is how trust is built and how followers come to feel like they truly know the person behind the posts.

As you engage with content from those you admire online, pay attention to the elements that draw you in and make you feel connected. These are the hallmarks of effective personal branding, serving as both inspiration and illustration of the power of presenting one's authentic self in the digital space.

This seamless integration of personal branding and copywriting significantly enhances audience engagement. When readers encounter copy that echoes a familiar voice and values, it ignites a sense of kinship and trust. They are not just engaging with content; they are engaging with you. This connection turns passive readers into active participants, more likely to comment, share and, ultimately, convert into loyal customers and clients. Your personal brand, expressed through your copy, becomes a magnet for like-minded individuals drawn to your authenticity and what you stand for.

The impact of personal branding on copywriting is profound. It elevates your writing from just words on a page to a powerful tool for building relationships, trust and engagement. As we go deeper into how you can use this power for your own small business, we'll explore strategies for aligning your personal brand with your copywriting efforts, ensuring that every word you write not only communicates your message, but amplifies your voice in the crowded digital marketplace.

3
Creating Your Personal Brand

Taking the leap into personal branding is not just about image; it is about digging deep into the essence of who you are, what you believe in and how you want to be seen. It is about laying down a foundation of your core values and unique selling propositions (USPs), which are the very elements that define the unique blend of you.

However, it's crucial to understand that your personal brand isn't solely defined by how you view yourself or even by the meticulous details you choose to broadcast. Instead, it comes to life in the minds of your audience through their interactions with your content, their perceptions of your public demeanour and the emotional responses you evoke in them. This is where the concept of branding becomes a two-way interaction rather than a one-sided declaration.

Your audience plays a decisive role in shaping your personal brand because branding, at its core, is perceptual. While you can suggest and imply through your communications and actions, it is ultimately up to your audience to interpret and define what your brand stands for. This interpretation is influenced by countless variables, including individual experiences, cultural backgrounds and personal biases, which means that each member of your audience may perceive your brand slightly differently.

And while you cannot control perception outright, you can influence it. This is done through consistent, strategic communication that aligns with the core values and USPs you've identified. Every blog post, tweet, presentation and interaction serves as a brush stroke in the broader painting of your brand. By consistently demonstrating qualities like integrity, expertise and innovation, you help shape how your audience sees you.

For example, if one of your core values is transparency, regularly sharing behind-the-scenes insights into your business processes or decision-making can reinforce this value in the eyes of your audience. Similarly, if innovation is a USP, showcasing your involvement in cutting-edge projects or your commitment to adopting new technologies can help cement this aspect of your brand.

The most effective way to guide perceptions is through authenticity. People have a keen sense for inauthenticity, and a brand that feels contrived or manipulative can push audiences away. By being genuine in your interactions and consistent in your messaging, you build trust.

This trust is foundational in not only attracting an audience, but converting them into loyal followers or clients who believe in your brand and endorse it to others.

Engaging with your audience is also a vital part of shaping your brand. Feedback, whether it comes through comments, reviews or direct messages, provides critical insights into how your brand is perceived and what might need adjustment. This feedback loop can inform your strategy, helping you to refine your approach and more effectively influence how you are seen. Remember that personal branding is not a static process. As your career evolves, as market dynamics shift and as audience preferences change, your brand too will need to adapt. Keeping the pulse on how your audience perceives you allows you to evolve in ways that maintain your relevance and resonance with your audience, ensuring that your personal brand continues to grow and impact effectively.

During this ongoing journey of self-discovery and audience engagement, the importance of courage cannot be overstated. Really getting to know yourself, discovering what truly makes you unique, involves a significant amount of bravery. In a society that often pushes us towards fitting in, taking a moment to reflect upon and appreciate what sets us apart is essential. Understanding and embracing our unique qualities allows us to develop personal brands that are not only genuinely authentic but deeply engaging.

The risks of neglecting personal brand development

Overlooking the development of your personal brand is akin to silencing your own voice in the marketplace. Without a solid foundation of a well-defined personal brand, your messages risk becoming generic, lacking the depth needed to truly resonate with your audience. This means you don't just miss opportunities, but you fail to make meaningful connections that could elevate your professional presence and impact.

The power of your personal brand extends directly into the effectiveness of your copy. A strong personal brand infuses your words with authenticity, making them more persuasive, relatable and impactful. More than that, it transforms your copy into a robust extension of your brand, imbued with the essence of your voice and the solidity of your values. This deep integration is crucial because it transforms your copy from just words to a compelling voice that acts as a magnet for your ideal audience.

While you can shape and suggest through your actions and communications, how your audience ultimately perceives your brand will colour their interactions with you. Crafting a personal brand with a clear foundation of authenticity and intent maximises the likelihood that audiences will see you as you intend to be seen. A genuine and transparent personal brand guides your audience into a deeper understanding and connection with you, potentially transforming casual followers into loyal clients.

But creating this kind of alignment isn't just about what you do outwardly. It is about looking inward. Being fearless with your personal brand means tackling not just the challenges others throw at you, but the ones you face within yourself. It is about questioning the stories you've been telling yourself about who you're supposed to be and having the courage to show your real self. This self-discovery is crucial. The more you know and accept about yourself, the more authentic and powerful your personal brand will be.

Being truly fearless involves overcoming both external and internal challenges. It is about defying the expectations and narratives that have been placed on you and embracing your genuine identity. The authenticity of your personal brand depends entirely on this deep understanding of yourself.

Identifying your core values and USPs

At the heart of a powerful personal brand are your core values and unique selling propositions (USPs). These elements are more than identifiers; they are the compelling story of what you stand for and what makes you different. They act as the magnetic core that attracts your ideal audience, stakeholders and collaborators.

Core values are your ethical compass, guiding every decision and interaction. They must be more than just words; they must be actionable and evident in all you do. For instance, if integrity is a core value, then transparency in your business practices should be non-negotiable. When your audience sees consistency between what you claim and what you practise, trust is built.

Here are some ways in which you can identify your core values:

1. Reflection on challenges and responses

Reflect on past challenges or situations where you felt a strong emotional response. What was at stake, and why did it matter so much to you? For instance, if you've ever stood up against a decision that felt unjust, perhaps fairness and justice are core values for you. Analysing these moments helps clarify what drives your actions and decisions at a fundamental level.

2. Passions and causes

Consider the causes or missions you are most passionate about. Whether it's environmental conservation, education or animal welfare, think about what these commitments say about your values. For example, if you're drawn to sustainability efforts, values like responsibility and stewardship might resonate with you.

3. Value selection exercises

Start with a broad list of values such as integrity, creativity, innovation, compassion and reliability. Select about ten that strike a chord with you. Then, challenge each by imagining scenarios where you might be pressured to compromise these values. Through this process, identify the top five that are absolutely non-negotiable. This exercise not only helps solidify what is most important to you, but prepares you to uphold these values under pressure.

To give you a clearer picture, here are some common core values and how they might manifest in a personal brand:

- **Integrity:** Consistently being honest and transparent in business practices; not just a claim but evident in your refusal to engage in misleading advertising or exaggerate claims about your services.
- **Compassion:** Actively supporting charitable causes or showing genuine concern for clients' challenges, reflecting a deep empathy in client relations and service delivery.
- **Innovation:** Continually pushing the boundaries of what is possible within your industry, regularly integrating the latest technologies or methodologies into your work.
- **Accountability:** Taking responsibility for your actions and their outcomes, which can be communicated through regular updates about business goals and the steps taken to achieve them.
- **Sustainability:** Prioritising environmental conservation in your operations, perhaps visible in your choice of materials, suppliers or even the topics you choose to discuss in public forums.

While it's essential to know and understand your core values, remember that articulating them to your audience doesn't always require direct statements. More effectively, your values should be evident through your actions and how you run your brand.

For example, if education is a core value, your content should consistently aim to inform and enlighten your audience, providing real value in each interaction. The companies and brands you choose to collaborate with should align with your values. For instance, partnering with eco-friendly brands can reinforce a commitment to sustainability. As another example, the way in which you handle client interactions can reflect values like respect, patience and integrity.

It is crucial to periodically assess whether your actions continue to align with your declared values. If feedback or self-reflection suggests a misalignment, consider this a critical juncture to realign your practices. If your audience can't easily identify your core values based on your brand's presence and actions, it might be time to make more explicit gestures or recalibrate your strategies to ensure these values shine through clearly and consistently.

Identifying and articulating your Unique Selling Proposition

Unique Selling Propositions (USPs) are the cornerstone of a compelling personal brand, serving as the definitive markers that distinguish you from the competition. They encapsulate the specific benefits and qualities that make your offerings superior or distinct from others in the market. In essence, USPs answer a critical question from potential clients or customers: "Why should I choose you?"

By clearly defining and communicating your USPs, you not only highlight what sets you apart, but define the unique value you provide. This clarity is essential not just for attracting attention in a crowded marketplace, but for building long-term relationships with your audience. USPs effectively communicate your brand's identity and promise, making them an integral part of how you connect with and retain your target audience.

Here are some ways in which you can identify your USPs:

1. Client feedback analysis

Start by engaging with the feedback you've received from past and current clients. This can be an invaluable source of insight into what aspects of your service or product feel special to them. Are they constantly praising a particular element of your service, such as your attention to detail or your innovative approach? Or perhaps they value your responsiveness and the personalised care they receive? Compile this feedback and look for patterns - these are indicators of your strong suits that naturally evolve into your USPs.

2. Competitive analysis

Examine your competitors closely. What are they offering, and how are they positioning themselves? More importantly, identify areas where they are lacking. Your USPs can often be found in the gaps left by others in your field. For instance, if most competitors in your niche overlook the importance of sustainable practices, and you use and promote eco-friendly materials, that's a potent USP. This analysis helps you understand where you can shine and differentiate yourself.

3. Leverage personal anecdotes

Your unique background and experiences can significantly influence your professional capabilities. For example, suppose you have a background in psychology and you're a copywriter. In that case, you might have a deeper understanding of how to craft messages that resonate emotionally with an audience, predicting and influencing consumer behaviour more effectively than your peers. These personal insights give your work a distinctive edge that can be a powerful USP.

4. Integration of unique skills or technology

Consider any special skills or technologies you use that enhance your offerings. For example, if you are using advanced analytics tools to refine marketing strategies, or perhaps you're skilled in a rare coding language that allows you to create uniquely functional websites, these are compelling USPs that appeal to a specific client base.

While it's essential to know your USPs, in a similar vein to your core values, broadcasting them explicitly isn't always necessary. Instead, they should be evident through the quality and characteristics of your work and how you engage with your market. Here is how to make sure they're clear to everyone who encounters your brand:

- Use your portfolio, if relevant to your field, to highlight projects that exemplify your USPs. If your USP is innovative problem-solving, showcase projects that demonstrate your ability to tackle and solve complex problems creatively.
- Incorporate detailed client testimonials and detailed case studies in your marketing materials. These not only validate your claims but highlight your USPs in action, showing potential clients the tangible benefits of working with you.
- Regularly produce content that reflects your USPs. If one of your USPs is a deep industry insight, publish reports, blog posts or newsletters that showcase your knowledge and keep your audience informed.

USPs are not set in stone; they evolve as your business grows and as market demands shift. Regularly revisit your USPs to ensure they still differentiate you effectively and resonate with your target audience. If you notice a shift in client feedback or market trends, be prepared to adapt your USPs to stay relevant and competitive.

This dynamic approach to understanding and implementing USPs requires a mix of introspection, market awareness and ongoing engagement with your audience. By deeply understanding and clearly demonstrating your unique values and capabilities, you create a personal brand that not only stands out but stands for something significant, appealing directly to the needs and desires of your ideal clients.

Messaging pillars and their relation to your personal brand

Messaging is a crucial aspect of personal branding, serving as the strategic foundation that supports and directs all communication efforts. Unlike content, which delivers your message, messaging shapes how your audience perceives and connects emotionally with your brand. Effective messaging ensures that your content doesn't just inform, but resonates, reflecting a cohesive brand identity that distinguishes your voice in the marketplace. This strategic alignment of what you say with your core values and unique selling propositions ensures a consistent and impactful brand presence. If your messaging pillars aren't immediately apparent to your audience, it indicates a misalignment in your branding strategy that needs addressing.

Messaging pillars form the thematic backbone of your brand's content strategy. These are the enduring themes that articulate your brand's mission, values and unique perspectives, and they should be clear to anyone who interacts with your brand. Effective messaging pillars encapsulate what you stand for, making your core values evident without needing to explicitly state them in every communication. A disconnect here suggests a deeper issue in conveying your brand's essence.

Developing messaging pillars involves:

1. Interest alignment

Combining your personal passions with your professional expertise is crucial in crafting a brand that is both authentic and engaging. This alignment ensures that your content is not only informative but infused with your unique enthusiasm and insight, making it more relatable and engaging to your audience.

Imagine you're a software developer with a deep interest in music. You could create content that explores the intersection of technology and music, such as developing music apps, the impact of artificial intelligence on music composition or reviews of tech products for musicians. This approach not only highlights your professional skills but your personal interests, giving your content a unique flavour that can differentiate your brand from others in tech.

2. Audience relevance

It is essential that your messaging resonates on a personal level with your audience. This means understanding their needs, challenges and aspirations, and tailoring your content to address these points. When your content directly speaks to your audience's concerns, it strengthens their connection to your brand, enhancing trust and loyalty.

For example, if your expertise is in retirement planning, your target audience likely includes individuals nearing retirement age who are concerned about their financial future. Your content could focus on topics like securing financial stability in retirement, investment strategies for retirees or how to maximise retirement benefits. Providing valuable information on these topics not only asserts your expertise, but directly addresses the core concerns of your audience.

3. Consistent content themes

Choosing consistent themes based on your messaging pillars ensures that your audience knows what to expect from your brand. This consistency helps in building a strong brand identity and credibility as it reassures your audience that they can rely on you for certain types of information or insight.

If one of your core values is sustainability, for example, your content should consistently reflect this. Whether you're a fashion brand or a business consultant, you can weave this value into your content by discussing sustainable practices within your industry, highlighting your own efforts to reduce environmental impact or showcasing sustainable products and services. For instance, a fashion blogger focusing on sustainability might feature eco-friendly fashion brands, provide tips for maintaining clothes longer or discuss the impact of the fashion industry on the environment. This not only underscores your commitment to sustainability, but aligns with the values of an audience that prioritises environmental consciousness.

In each of these examples, the key is not just the content itself, but how it reflects the core values and unique aspects of your personal brand. By consistently aligning your content with your personal interests, audience needs and thematic consistency, you not only make your brand more appealing and relatable but more memorable and influential in your field.

Identifying effective messaging pillars is an essential step in shaping a personal brand that communicates clearly and resonates deeply. These pillars serve as the backbone of your content strategy, ensuring each piece of content you produce not only aligns with your brand's mission but engages your audience meaningfully. Here are some strategies that can help you pinpoint these pillars, maintaining a narrative flow that ties back to the essence of personal branding:

1. Content audit

Begin by conducting a thorough review of your existing content. Look for patterns and themes that emerge naturally in what you've already created. Pay special attention to the types of engagement each piece of content receives. Which topics generate the most discussion? Which posts are shared the most? This reflection helps you understand what resonates with your audience and what aspects of your content could be developed into messaging pillars.

For instance, if you notice that your articles on productivity hacks consistently gain more traction and comments, this could indicate that your audience values practical, actionable advice in this area. Making productivity one of your core messaging pillars could therefore enhance audience engagement and brand relevance.

2. Market and audience insights

Take a detailed look into market trends and audience feedback. Use tools like social media analytics and client feedback forms to gather data on your audience's preferences and behaviours. What topics are currently trending in your industry? What issues are your audience members most vocal about? Aligning your messaging pillars with both emerging trends and audience interests ensures that your content stays relevant and appealing.

For example, if you're in the health and wellness space and there's a growing interest in mental health, incorporating this into your messaging pillars could attract a broader audience. This alignment not only showcases your brand's responsiveness to market shifts but strengthens its connection with audience concerns and needs.

3. Collaborative brainstorming

Regular brainstorming sessions with your team or with mentors can uncover fresh perspectives and innovative ideas. These collaborative efforts can bring out unique angles and insights that resonate with your brand's values and audience's expectations because you're tapping into collective creativity to find distinct voices and themes that could define your brand.

Consider a scenario where you and your team discuss how to differentiate your environmental consultancy from competitors. Through brainstorming, you might discover a unique approach, such as focusing on local community impacts of environmental policies, which could serve as a distinct messaging pillar that highlights your brand's unique perspective and expertise.

4. Strategic integration

Incorporating these identified pillars into your personal brand strategy is not about confining your creativity but about channelling it to build a strong, consistent identity. These pillars should guide your content creation, ensuring that every blog post, video or tweet not only contributes to a unified brand narrative but strengthens your position as an authority in your field.

By establishing clear, well-defined messaging pillars, you streamline your content strategy and enhance your brand's overall consistency. This strategic focus makes your messaging a potent tool for building genuine connections and extending your influence in your professional sphere. Ultimately, these pillars do not restrict your creativity; rather, they provide a framework within which your creativity can thrive, ensuring every piece of content you produce is purposeful and impactful.

Finding your brand voice

As we near the end of this chapter, let's talk about the journey of establishing your brand voice. This is fundamentally about infusing your communications with a consistent and identifiable personality that mirrors your core values, USPs and messaging pillars. This voice acts not merely as an echo of your brand's identity but as a defining element that makes your brand both relatable and memorable.

Your brand voice should be an authentic extension of your persona or the carefully crafted character that represents your brand. This involves a thoughtful alignment of your natural communication style with the expectations of your audience. If your personal style is naturally informal but your target audience values a more refined approach, finding a balance that remains true to your personality while appealing to your audience's preferences is crucial.

For example, consider a financial consultant with a penchant for informal dialogue, aiming to demystify complex financial concepts for young adults. This professional might adopt a conversational yet informative tone, using simple explanations and relatable analogies, thus making high-level finance more accessible and engaging.

The tone of your communication should consistently reflect your brand's underlying values and mission across all platforms. This doesn't mean every piece of content sounds the same, but rather they all should feel like they come from the same source. For instance, even when addressing serious topics, a brand known for its light-hearted approach can maintain its voice by weaving in appropriate humour or a hopeful outlook.

Consider the idea that a children's educational brand might tackle various subjects from basic arithmetic to bullying. Regardless of the topic, the tone remains nurturing, encouraging and optimistic, reinforcing the brand's commitment to positive, child-friendly learning.

Selecting appropriate language involves tuning into your audience's linguistic preferences while staying faithful to your brand's character. This means not only choosing words that resonate with your audience but constructing messages that reflect your unique perspective.

A tech startup aiming to attract a young, innovative crowd, for example, might incorporate current tech slang and industry jargon that resonates with a tech-savvy audience, making the brand feel current and knowledgeable.

Your brand voice, while needing consistency, should also be flexible enough to evolve as your brand grows and as audience dynamics shift. This evolution is a sign of a brand's responsiveness to change, a quality that can significantly strengthen your audience's loyalty. Regularly scheduled reviews of your brand voice can ensure that it remains effective and relevant. These reviews can coincide with broader market analysis or internal reviews of brand strategy.

Crafting and maintaining a brand voice is an iterative and nuanced process that goes beyond mere content creation; it is about creating and nurturing a deep connection with your audience through every word you share. This connection is built on the pillars of authenticity, consistency and adaptability, ensuring that your brand not only communicates effectively but leaves a lasting impression. Remember, the ultimate goal is not just to be heard, but to be understood and valued, building a loyal community around your brand.

Creating a fearless personal brand

As we culminate our exploration into establishing a robust personal brand, it's vital to anchor these insights back to the core theme of our journey together: embracing fearlessness. Crafting your brand is more than a strategic endeavour; it is a courageous act of presenting your authentic self to the world. This authenticity can be daunting; indeed, it demands a level of vulnerability that many find intimidating.

The idea of showcasing your true self and your real values to the world can be frightening. You may worry about judgement, rejection or simply not being good enough in the eyes of your audience. Yet, it's this very authenticity that cultivates deep connections and builds trust. When your audience recognises the genuine passion and honesty in your voice, you don't just communicate; you resonate.

Being fearless with your words means more than being bold in your choice of language or daring in your marketing strategies. It involves a profound willingness to let your true self be seen. This doesn't mean you must reveal every aspect of your personal life or every thought you have; rather, it's about aligning your public communications so closely with your values and passions that anyone interacting with your brand feels the integrity and sincerity behind your words.

From a practical standpoint, a genuine brand voice also enhances your sales strategy. When people trust you, they are more likely to buy from you. Authenticity in your voice ensures that your sales pitches are not just pitches; they are conversations. They are invitations to your audience to join you in something bigger – a movement, a journey, a community. This approach transforms potential transactions into engagements of shared values and common goals.

Developing your brand voice isn't just a tactic; it is a commitment to truth in advertising, to integrity in marketing and to authenticity in every piece of content you create. It is about being bold enough to stand out and wise enough to speak your truth. The fear of authenticity is real, but the rewards of overcoming this fear - deep connections, authentic influence and meaningful sales - are immense. My challenge to you at the end of this chapter is to embrace this journey with open arms. Let your brand voice be a fearless expression of who you are and what you stand for. Remember, in a world crowded with disingenuity, a voice that dares to be true is the voice that leaves a lasting impact. This is your opportunity not just to be heard, but to truly connect and transform your audience with every word you write.

4

Communicating Fearlessly for Influence and Sales

It is now time to take a deeper look into the nuanced art of content creation. This is where your personal brand's voice is not merely heard but profoundly felt. This is where we transmute the raw materials of your identity – your core values, unique selling propositions and messaging pillars – into a compelling narrative that does more than capture attention; it resonates, influences and converts.

When it comes to digital communication, authenticity is your beacon. It is what makes your content not only seen but deeply experienced by your audience. Authentic content transcends the mere act of sharing knowledge or selling a product or service; it is an open invitation into your world. It reflects your struggles, celebrates your victories and, most importantly, it showcases your unwavering truths.

Writing content that embodies your authentic self can seem daunting in the noisy streets of social media and the wider online world that often rewards the loudest voices. Yet, it is the quiet yet consistent authenticity that really creates lasting connections and builds legacies. This chapter aims to empower you to weave your personal narratives into your content strategically, allowing your audience to connect not just with your brand, but with you as a person.

Embracing fearlessness in your content strategy

To be fearless is to acknowledge your fears, confront them and use them as forces of empowerment. In the context of content creation, this means daring to tackle topics that resonate deeply with you, even when they challenge the mainstream narratives. It involves articulating bold opinions and maintaining integrity in your values, even when market trends suggest a contrary path.

We will explore how to identify the specific fears that may be diluting your content's impact - be it fear of criticism, fear of not conforming or fear of revealing too much - and how these fears can be transformed into powerful catalysts for leaving a real impact on your audience. This section will provide you with tools not only to face your fears, but to allow them to guide you in creating content that truly stands out.

It is important to note that engagement is the bridge between your content and your audience. This section of the chapter will focus on practical strategies to captivate your audience from the first line. You will learn how to maintain interest through a compelling narrative and how to motivate action with a persuasive call to action. These techniques extend beyond basic writing skills; they are about imbuing your content with the passion of your convictions and the clarity of your purpose.

We will dissect various methods to hook readers, maintain their interest and guide them towards a meaningful interaction with your brand. From crafting intriguing openings to delivering satisfying conclusions, every element of your content will be honed to reflect your brand's unique voice and mission.

Additionally, we'll explore how to adapt your core message across these formats without losing the essence of your personal brand. This adaptability is key in reaching diverse audiences and enhancing your brand's reach.

Fearlessness in content creation also involves the courage to scrutinise your work critically. So the final section of this chapter will guide you through using analytics and feedback not as deterrents, but as tools for growth and refinement. You will learn how to interpret engagement metrics, understand what they mean for your content strategy and how to use this information to refine and evolve your approach.

Measuring success isn't just about applauding what worked; it is about understanding why something didn't and learning how to adapt. By embracing this iterative process, you ensure that your content strategy remains dynamic, responsive and continually aligned with your brand's core values and objectives.

By the end of this chapter, you will be equipped not only to create content that resonates with your identity, but to do so with strategic brilliance and fearless authenticity. This is all about moulding your voice into a symphony that doesn't just make noise, but really resonates in the hearts and minds of your audience. This is how you turn the fear of expression into the art of influence, transforming every word you write into a step towards profound connections and lasting impact.

Confronting and using fear to amplify your content's impact

In the nuanced world of digital communication, fear often looms like an uninvited guest, whispering doubts and exaggerating our deepest insecurities. Yet, this unwelcome presence harbours unexpected gifts: the potential to deepen the impact of our storytelling, enrich our message and enhance our influence. By acknowledging and understanding our fears, we transform them into potent forces that not only challenge us but compel us to present our most authentic selves.

Let me share with you moments from my own journey, where fears not only surfaced but momentarily seemed to hold the upper hand. Each of these experiences, while initially daunting, ultimately reinforced the resilience and authenticity of my personal brand.

1. The fear of divisive opinions

I once decided to share my thoughts on a somewhat controversial topic. It was a subject I felt passionately about, one that aligned closely with my core values. However, the moment I clicked 'post', a flutter of anxiety stirred within me. What if my audience disagreed? What if this sparked backlash? The reactions were mixed. Some disagreed, a few comments were sharply critical, but here's what mattered: it sparked a conversation. It was just an opinion, after all. *My* opinion. And the disagreement didn't redefine my worth or the value of my message. It was a clear demonstration that diverse opinions can coexist, each adding to the discourse. This experience taught me that standing by your values, even in the face of potential conflict, reinforces the authenticity of your brand and can significantly deepen the engagement with your audience.

2. The fear of personal attacks

In another instance, I attached a personal photo to a social media post, aiming to leverage social media algorithms better. It was one of the first times I'd shared a full-body photograph of myself, having hidden my body for much of my online career until then. The post did well in terms of reach, but not all feedback was kind. Among the supportive messages were comments critiquing my appearance, harsh words that stung. I was called, amongst many things, 'fat' - a comment intended to wound. A comment that stirred difficult memories of the bullying I experienced as a teenager. Yet, here was a crucial real connection: their words reflected their perspectives and limitations, not mine. This incident didn't define me but highlighted a vital brand truth: vulnerability in sharing personal aspects can lead to both support and criticism. However, true strength lies in continuing to present oneself authentically, understanding that while not everyone will be your ideal client or follower, those who resonate with your truth will stand steadfastly by you.

3. The fear of being told 'you're wrong'

Sharing causes and beliefs that are close to your heart is another area where fear often whispers louder. I once shared my support for a cause I believed deeply in. The backlash was immediate - some insisted that my views were wrong. Yet, what is 'right' and 'wrong' in personal conviction? This experience underscored a fundamental lesson: you are not for everyone, and that's not just okay; it is necessary. If you speak from a place aligned with your brand, values and mission, then you are speaking your truth. Those who are meant to connect with your message will do so, and those who aren't will not and should not deter you from your path.

Each of these instances of fear, while undeniably challenging, were invaluable. They were not merely obstacles but opportunities, moments that demanded a choice: retract or expand. By choosing to lean into the fear, letting it guide rather than govern, I found a richer, more resonant voice. I've used these instances of fear to remind myself to move *with* it rather than try to fight against it ever since.

Being vulnerable enough to share your authentic self, embrace potential criticism and stand by your convictions are acts of courage. It invites others to engage with you at a deeper level and inspires them to also embrace their fears. The reality is that no one is truly fearless. Fearlessness is a practice, an ongoing challenge that we rise to meet day after day in our personal and professional lives.

This journey through fear is about transformation. It is about understanding that the very things that scare us also fuel our growth. They compel us to be honest, be real and connect in ways that mere surface-level interaction never will. When we practise fearlessness, we don't just change the narrative of our content; we change the impact of our presence.

Let your fears inform you, not define you. They are not indicators of your limits but signposts towards growth. As you continue to navigate the complexities of creating authentic content, let your fears be your guide, not your guard. Allow them to open you to new levels of engagement, deeper connections with your audience and, ultimately, a brand that stands out not just for what it says, but for the truth and courage it represents.

Transforming fear into a creative catalyst

We are *all* scared. Yet, within fear lies a tremendous opportunity - to transform it into a creative catalyst that not only elevates our work but connects us more deeply with our audience. This transformation demands a deliberate recalibration of our perspective, a shift from seeing fear as a formidable foe to embracing it as an ally in our creative journey.

My journey with fear began in the echoes of harsh feedback. Each critique felt like a personal slight, an arrow striking at the heart of my identity. However, the real transformation came when I chose to reframe these experiences. I began to see each piece of criticism not as a weapon but as a tool, sculpting my skills and refining my message.

This shift was far from easy. It required me to dissect my fears, sit with them, understand their roots and ultimately redefine them. I learned to appreciate criticism for what it truly was - an opportunity for growth and improvement. This reframing wasn't just about changing my thoughts but about reshaping my entire approach to content creation. It led to a resilience that now underpins my work, urging me to push beyond the comfortable and the known into a space where true innovation can thrive.

The fear of revealing too much of myself was another barrier. What if my personal insights alienated my audience? What if my true voice wasn't what they wanted to hear? The strategy I employed was one of incremental exposure, slowly weaving more personal anecdotes and insights into my content.

Each step was measured, each story shared was a test of the waters. This methodical approach allowed me to gauge how my authenticity affected engagement. To my surprise, with each small reveal, the feedback grew more positive, the connections deeper. The incremental exposure built not just my audience's trust, but my confidence. It showed me that the unique aspects of my voice were not just accepted but appreciated.

Perhaps the most profound lesson came when I decided to openly share a particularly painful part of my journey. This was an exercise in vulnerability that I approached with great trepidation. However, the response was overwhelmingly positive. People didn't see my challenges as flaws but as proof of my perseverance. They didn't view my admissions as weaknesses but as acts of courage. This vulnerability helped form a bond with my audience that went beyond the superficial layers of typical brand-consumer relationships, and from it a community of support, encouragement and mutual growth was created.

As we navigate the world of digital marketing and content creation, transforming fear is not just about altering our output; it fundamentally changes our relationship with our audience. My own journey of grappling with the fear of criticism illustrates this transformation well. Initially, every critique felt like a personal attack, reinforcing my self-doubt. However, by shifting my perspective to see criticism as an opportunity for growth, I began to approach each piece of content with the mindset that it should not only inform but inspire. This pursuit of excellence ensures that the work I put forth isn't merely adequate; it strives to be exceptional, worthy of the trust and time invested by those who engage with it.

Embracing my unique perspective was another crucial step in my evolution. The fear of standing out - of not conforming - once seemed daunting. By facing this fear and embracing my individuality, my distinctive voice began to emerge, defining the essence of my brand. This authentic expression did not isolate me. Instead, it carved out a specific niche that attracted an audience craving originality and depth.

Opening up about my vulnerabilities transformed my relationship with my audience from a formal exchange to a genuine connection. Initially, I perceived vulnerability as a risk, exposing myself to judgement. Yet, sharing my personal experiences, the struggles and triumphs, not only solidified the authenticity of my brand but invited my audience to see their reflections in my story, deepening our connection.

To integrate fear positively into my creative process, I embraced several practical strategies. Constructing feedback loops became part of my routine, actively seeking and engaging with my audience's reactions to refine and improve my content. Regular content audits are crucial, helping identify what truly resonates, guiding my future projects and ensuring that my messages remain relevant as the needs and contexts of my audience evolve.

Participating in relevant communities has also been invaluable, providing a safe space where fears and aspirations are shared. These communities offer support and inspire new ideas, which creates an environment where we learn from each other's journeys, not in competition but in camaraderie.

Through these approaches, fear becomes more than a hurdle to overcome – it transforms into a force that drives innovation, enhances engagement and creates genuine connections. As we tread our creative paths, will you join me in actively and audaciously not shying away from the fears that confront us? Join me instead in embracing and transforming them into elements that not only communicate but connect and resonate on a profoundly human level.

As we wrap up this exploration into walking alongside fear to amplify the impact of your content, we find ourselves at a crucial juncture. Fear, when channelled effectively, can indeed transform our communications, pushing us beyond mere expression to true connection. But this transformation isn't merely about mastering the mechanics of content creation; it is about taking a much deeper look at the essence of what makes our communications resonate on a fundamentally human level. This resonance is grounded in authenticity – the raw, unfiltered expression of who we are.

As we transition from understanding how to shape fear into a powerful tool for truly impactful content, let us turn our focus towards the core of impactful communication: authenticity. The next chapter explores how genuine authenticity not only elevates our message, but transforms our entire approach to digital communication, developing connections that extend beyond fleeting interactions to lasting relationships and, of course, sales.

5
The Essence of Authentic Content

In the previous chapter, we explored the dynamics of fear in shaping content, learning to use it as a catalyst for creativity and engagement. Building on that foundation, this chapter shifts our focus to a critical component that not only complements but transcends every aspect of content creation: authenticity. Here, we uncover how infusing our content with genuine personal insights and experiences does more than capture attention; it creates a bridge between our world and that of our audience, creating a deeper connection that is the hallmark of truly influential communication.

Authenticity is not just about being real; it is about being relatable. It is about allowing your audience to see themselves in your story, to feel their own fears, aspirations and joys reflected in your words. This chapter is dedicated to unlocking the power of authenticity in your digital communication, transforming routine interactions into meaningful exchanges that resonate deeply and drive engagement.

Authenticity isn't just a strategic approach but the foundation of a connection that endures and impacts profoundly. When you choose to infuse your content with the raw, unedited essence of who you are - your struggles, your victories, your ongoing journey - you invite your audience into a world where they can see their reflections in your story. This isn't just content creation; it is a form of bonding that extends beyond conventional marketing into the realm of genuine relationship-building.

Authentic content does more than inform; it transforms. It bridges the gap between individual experiences and collective understanding, turning personal insights into universal truths that resonate across your audience. But achieving this level of authenticity requires more than just the willingness to share; it demands courage. The courage to delve deep into your personal and professional ethos, peel back the polished layers of your brand and reveal the human core beneath.

Now let us look at some actionable steps for writing truly authentic content.

1. Narrative storytelling

Begin by mining your past and present for stories that paint a vivid picture of your journey. Do not shy away from the lows; it is in these moments that your resilience shines brightest. Narrate how each challenge shaped you and how overcoming them fortified your vision. This narrative style not only enhances engagement but builds a character arc that your audience can root for. To leverage this effectively in copywriting:

- Structure your story by using a classic narrative flow (beginning, middle, end) to outline your content. Start with a hook that grabs attention, explain the conflict or challenge, and conclude with a resolution that leaves your audience inspired or reflective.
- Incorporate sensory details so that your stories are more vivid by using descriptive language that appeals to the senses. This technique helps paint a clearer picture and makes your narrative more immersive. For example, instead of simply stating, "I worked late into the night," you could enhance it by adding, "as the clock ticked past midnight, the soft glow of my laptop was the only light in the room, echoing the loneliness of my struggle."
- Showing vulnerability is powerful, so share personal anecdotes that showcase your failures and doubts as well as your successes. This can make you more relatable and trustworthy, which are key components of influencing decisions and building loyalty.

2. Value integration

Each piece of content you produce should be a testament to the values that define your brand. Whether it's through a blog post, a video or a simple tweet, ensure that the core values of integrity, innovation or community resonate through. This consistent reinforcement of values not only solidifies your brand's identity but attracts an audience whose values align with yours. To do this effectively:

- Highlight value-driven stories. What I mean by this is to share examples from your business practices where your core values guided your decisions. For instance, if one of your values is community, describe a specific instance where you chose a community-focused solution over a more profitable, yet less communal-friendly option.
- Use value-laden language, so choose words and phrases that reflect your values consistently across all your content. If innovation is a key value, use terms like 'cutting-edge', 'pioneering' or 'trailblazing' to reinforce this value subtly through your language choices.
- Create value-based content themes that explore your values in action. For example, a series on 'innovation in action' could feature case studies, interviews or analyses that showcase how innovation is integral to your operations and offerings.

3. Reflective engagement

Tailor your content to mirror the aspirations and challenges of your audience. This means going beyond demographic data to understand the psychographic makeup of your followers. What drives them? What keeps them up at night? Use this insight to create content that speaks directly to their experiences, thereby deepening their connection to your brand. Implement this by:

- Developing detailed audience personas based on psychographic and demographic research. Use these personas to tailor your content, addressing specific fears, desires and scenarios relevant to each persona.
- Using quizzes, surveys or simple question posts that require audience input. These formats can be designed to reflect the audience's outcomes based on their inputs, which makes the content personalised and more engaging.
- Regularly soliciting feedback through social media polls, comments or direct messages and showing how this feedback influences your content and business practices. This not only makes your audience feel heard but deepens their engagement by involving them in the content creation process.

Implementing these advanced storytelling and copywriting techniques involves a thoughtful blend of creativity, strategic planning and ongoing interaction with your audience. Start by selecting one or two key strategies that align closely with your brand's current goals and audience insights. Experiment with different formats and track engagement metrics to see what resonates most with your audience. Over time, refine your approach based on the data and feedback collected and consider integrating more complex strategies as your brand's storytelling prowess grows.

In essence, transforming your copywriting through advanced storytelling is not just about selling a product or service; it is about creating a narrative experience that builds genuine connections, creates a sense of trust and positions your brand as an influential presence in the lives of your audience.

The psychological foundations of empathetic storytelling in copywriting

Empathetic storytelling is more than a narrative technique; it is a psychological strategy that taps into the core of human experience, creating a profound connection between the storyteller and the listener – or in the case of marketing, between the brand and the consumer. This connection is not merely aesthetic; it is deeply psychological, tapping into emotions and shared experiences to drive influence and increase sales. Let's explore why empathetic storytelling holds such power and how it can be effectively utilised in copywriting.

1. Emotional resonance

Humans are emotional beings, driven by feelings as much as, if not more than, logic. When a story makes us feel something – joy, sadness, hope, fear – it creates a stronger and longer-lasting impression. This emotional engagement is crucial in marketing as it helps to imprint a brand into the consumer's memory.

2. Mirror neurons

Neuroscientific research suggests the presence of 'mirror neurons' in our brains, which react not only when we perform an action but when we observe the same action performed by someone else. This means that when we see someone experiencing something in a story, our neurons fire as if we were experiencing it ourselves. This neurological mirroring can make empathetic storytelling an incredibly powerful tool for influencing and persuading an audience.

3. Cognitive empathy

Effective storytelling often utilises cognitive empathy: the ability to understand another's perspective or mental state. When a brand can demonstrate that it truly understands and empathises with its audience's challenges or desires, it builds trust. Trust is foundational in converting casual interest into lasting loyalty and can directly influence buying decisions.

Empathetic storytelling leverages several psychological triggers:

- **Relatability:** When stories feature characters or scenarios that audiences can see themselves in, the content becomes more engaging and persuasive. This relatability increases the audience's investment in the narrative outcome, which can be aligned with product or service solutions offered by the brand.
- **Aspirational drivers:** People are often driven by who they aspire to be, not just who they are. Stories that align with audience aspirations can motivate actions towards becoming that ideal self, which often includes purchasing decisions that align with that desired identity.

- **Social proof:** Integrating stories of other customers or clients who have successfully used a product or service acts as social proof, a powerful influencer in consumer behaviour. Seeing others' success lowers perceived risk and can trigger a 'bandwagon effect', where people are influenced to engage in behaviours simply because others are doing so.
- **Conflict and resolution:** A story's appeal often lies in its dramatic arc – introducing a conflict and then resolving it. In marketing, presenting a product or service as the resolution to a conflict not only highlights its necessity but its effectiveness, encouraging purchase behaviour.

In the current digital age where consumers are bombarded with countless marketing messages, those that feel genuine are the ones that stand out. Authenticity in storytelling means sharing true stories with real emotional cores, not just fabricated narratives designed to manipulate.

Incorporating empathetic storytelling into your content transforms it from mere information dissemination into powerful, emotionally resonant messages that engage, persuade and convert. This approach leverages deep psychological principles to not only capture attention but drive both influence and sales, making it a cornerstone technique for any marketer looking to elevate their brand in the hearts and minds of their audience.

Lettuce reconsider the hidden power of the mundane

Having explored the profound psychological impact of empathetic storytelling, we now turn to a nuanced aspect of authenticity that many overlook: the value of the mundane. Often, it's the simplest parts of our lives, the ones we deem too 'boring' to share, that most deeply resonate with others.

One of the most pervasive fears in personal branding is the belief that our own stories are not compelling enough to share, that they are too mundane, too 'boring' to capture anyone's attention. This fear is not only misguided but dismissive of a fundamental truth in human connection: relatability is the cornerstone of genuine engagement. Stories deemed 'boring' – those encapsulating everyday challenges, modest joys and universal experiences – often wield the most power. They act as a mirror, reflecting the shared human condition, thus creating a deep sense of understanding and solidarity.

Consider my now famous lettuce tale, a saga that unfolded from a simple trip to the supermarket and ended up resonating with hundreds. The story began innocently enough, with my husband and I navigating a packed Lidl car park. As we transferred our groceries into the cab (we don't drive, which is itself a tale for another day) one of our bags succumbed to the weight of too many middle-aisle treasures and split right open.

As various items made a break for it, rolling towards impending doom beneath car tyres, my husband frantically scrambled to salvage what he could, while I focused on securing the remaining bags. Pure chaos.

However, the chaos found its peak when, while unpacking, I realised we were missing a crucial player in our dinner plans: the lettuce. Despite the heroic efforts of my husband, the lettuce had vanished, presumably rolling into the night (or perhaps into the boot of our cab). I shared this ordeal in an email to my subscribers, framing it not just as a humorous misadventure but as a metaphor for the essential elements we often overlook in our businesses.

The response was unexpected. My inbox was flooded with replies – not just acknowledgements and sympathy for the loss of a crucial dinner ingredient, but shared stories of similar, trivial mishaps that struck a chord. This simple narrative of a lost head of lettuce did more than give my audience a laugh; it sparked a connection over the shared experiences of life's small chaos. What resonated wasn't the missing vegetable itself, but the humour and humanity in such a mundane mishap. It wasn't just about a lost piece of produce; it was about finding common ground in our all-too-human moments of forgetfulness and frustration. This story, though trivial, underscored a profound business lesson shared in the same email: just as a burger feels incomplete without a crisp slice of lettuce, a business can feel incomplete without its unique offerings fully articulated and presented.

The reality is, the mundane aspects of your story are incredibly potent. In these everyday details, your audience finds common ground, sees potential for change and feels deeply understood. Yes, even when the story revolves around a lettuce! These narratives ground your brand in a relatable reality and enhance its accessibility. By embracing and sharing these ordinary yet relatable experiences, you not only humanise your brand but deepen the connection with your audience, making your brand not just seen but really felt.

Bridging the gap between the simplicity of our everyday actions and the overarching narrative of our brand's mission can reveal a profound layer of engagement. So as we take a deeper look at the storytelling potential within the fabric of our daily operations, let us explore how these routines are not merely tasks to be completed, but stories to be told.

Giving your audience a look into the daily rhythms of a solo entrepreneur or small business owner offers a unique narrative opportunity that can profoundly resonate with your ideal clients. From the early morning rituals that set the tone for the day to the quiet satisfaction of shutting down after a productive session, these routines are not just tasks; they embody the essence of your brand's dedication and passion.

For instance, consider how a simple Zoom meeting might spark a transformative idea, or how an email exchange with a client can evolve from a routine interaction to a heartfelt discussion that ends with valuable feedback and mutual appreciation. When you share these moments, focusing on the emotional dynamics - such as the anticipation of presenting a new proposal or the joy in resolving a client's issue - you not only engage but form a deeper connection with your audience. This connection is critical as it transforms your brand from a service provider into a trusted partner and ally.

Your daily practices, when narrated thoughtfully, reveal the craftsmanship and meticulous attention that define your operations. Describing how you organise your workspace, choose your tools and software or even select your projects can shed light on the precision and care that go into every aspect of your business. These details, though seemingly mundane, highlight your commitment to quality and efficiency, resonating with clients who value attention to detail.

Challenges are an integral part of any business narrative. Sharing how you navigate these hurdles - such as troubleshooting a technical glitch or handling an unexpected delay - can illustrate your resourcefulness and resilience. By detailing how you approach and solve these issues, you humanise your brand and demonstrate your adaptability, qualities that are highly appealing to potential clients.

Creativity often flourishes in the least expected moments. Whether it's devising a new approach to streamline an administrative task or brainstorming a fresh marketing angle, these sparks of innovation are stories worth telling. They showcase that creativity isn't confined to major projects or breakthroughs; it is woven into the fabric of everyday business life, enhancing your narrative with layers of ingenuity and proactive thinking.

Interactions with clients provide a goldmine of stories with great potential for deepening relationships. For example, a client's suggestion might lead you to refine a product, which not only improves the offering but cements a loyal relationship. Such narratives not only underscore your openness to feedback but your commitment to evolving with your clients' needs.

Linking these daily anecdotes to the broader narrative of your brand helps illuminate how ordinary tasks align with your core values, like commitment to client satisfaction or continuous improvement. A story about organising your digital files, for instance, might seem trivial, but when told as part of your commitment to operational excellence, it gains new significance.

Reflecting on the genesis of your brand - recalling the early challenges and the pivotal moments of clarity - can provide a compelling contrast to your current successes. These origin stories resonate widely, offering inspiration and demonstrating the growth and perseverance at the heart of your brand. Each mundane moment, each routine task performed by you or your small team, contributes to the narrative of your brand. Highlighting these efforts showcases not just a business operation but a living, breathing entity powered by individuals dedicated to their craft. This perspective shifts the view of your brand from a simple business to a dynamic community of motivated professionals.

In crafting these stories, focus on the sensory and emotional details that bring these experiences to life. This narrative approach does more than document; it captivates, inviting your audience to see the ordinary through an extraordinary lens. Listening to how your audience responds to these stories and letting their feedback inform your narrative turns your content strategy into a dynamic dialogue that brings about genuine engagement and influence. Through this ongoing exchange, you build not just a brand, but a legacy that resonates with authenticity and heartfelt connection.

Embracing authenticity in every fibre of your brand

As we conclude our exploration of authentic content, we reflect upon the transformative power of genuine connections. Throughout this chapter, we've taken a detailed look at the essence of narrative storytelling, the integration of core values and the strategic engagement with our audience, all of which are fundamental in creating content that resonates on a profound level.

We have seen how authenticity doesn't just enrich the content; it transforms it, making every interaction an opportunity for meaningful connection. This connection is pivotal, for it lays the groundwork for the next crucial step in our entrepreneurial journey: converting engagement into sales. The courage to share our true selves, the creativity to weave compelling narratives and the commitment to embody our values have consistently prepared us to confidently step into the arena of sales. The authenticity we've nurtured is not just a tool for storytelling, but a powerful catalyst for salesmanship.

In the upcoming chapter, we'll pivot from the philosophical underpinnings of content creation to the practical dynamics of sales. We will explore how to use the authentic connections we've built to fearlessly ask for the sale. You will learn sophisticated techniques to write sales copy that not only speaks to the mind but resonates with the heart, employing empathy and assertiveness in measures that compel action.

Prepare to transform the trust and rapport built and developed through your authentic content into successful conversions. We will dissect how to articulate compelling calls to action, balance persuasion with genuineness and, ultimately, how to make every word count not just in telling stories but in sealing deals.

Let's carry forward the integrity and impact of our content into the mastery of sales, where the true measure of our communication's effectiveness will be tested and proven. As we move forward, remember, the authenticity that has defined our content is the same authenticity that will redefine our sales approach, making not just a statement, making not just money, but making a real difference.

6
The Courage to Ask for the Sale and Convert

As we've journeyed together through the art of writing authentic content, we've learnt that each story shared, every vulnerability embraced, doesn't just capture attention but cultivates profound connections. We have peeled back layers, revealing not just the surface of our professional personas but the pulsing, vibrant life beneath. We have seen how our true selves can resonate deeply, building bridges of trust and understanding with those who encounter our work.

Up to this point, we've explored what it means to be truly authentic, diving into the profound ways our real stories engage and bind us to our audience. We have tackled the fears that shape our creative expressions, turning everyday insights into compelling narratives that draw people closer to the core of what we do and who we are. Now, poised at this critical juncture, we stand ready to bridge the delicate gap between creating a connection with our audience and achieving tangible business outcomes – sales.

The leap from creating content to converting it into sales might seem daunting, a shift from the soulful art of connection to the stark mechanics of commerce. Yet, this transition need not be a departure from our authenticity. Instead, it can be its boldest affirmation. Fear often surrounds the act of selling, rooted in worries that asking for the sale might undermine the genuine connections we've nurtured. But what if selling is viewed not as a compromise but as a continuation of the conversation, a chance to affirm the value we believe our work truly holds?

This chapter invites you to redefine the essence of selling within the framework of your authentic narrative. It is not merely about transactions; it is about offering a piece of your vision, a fragment of your passion, a solution infused with your expertise and care. Selling in this light becomes an extension of the dialogue already flourishing between you and your audience, an opportunity to deepen engagement and deliver on the promises your content has made.

As we journey into the nuanced strategies that transform authentic engagement into effective sales, remember, each technique, each principle and each example is rooted deeply in the authenticity we've championed from the start. You are not merely peddling a product or service; you are extending an invitation into your vision, sharing a solution that bears the weight of your expertise and passion. I encourage you to approach this chapter not just as a sales guide but as a manifesto for courageously genuine engagement in every aspect of your business dealings.

Step into the world of sales with a refreshed perspective, armed with the conviction that your authenticity is not just a part of your brand; it is your most potent selling point. I am now going to show you how to ask for the sale with integrity and confidence, ensuring your calls to action resonate as powerfully as your stories. This is not just about making more money but about validating the worth of what you've created. I hope that by the end of this chapter you will have started to see selling as an act of bold, authentic invitation, transforming interest into enthusiastic commitment and turning those genuine connections you've worked so hard to create into lasting successes that make a significant impact on your bank account.

Understanding the psychology of sales

Before we begin the next phase of our journey – translating those authentic connections into successful sales – it is essential to grasp the underlying psychological triggers that influence purchasing decisions. At the core of every transaction lies a complex interplay of emotions, needs and desires, all woven into the very fabric of human behaviour. Understanding these elements can dramatically enhance how we approach sales, ensuring that our efforts resonate deeply and genuinely with potential buyers.

The psychology of sales is not just about understanding what prompts someone to buy; it is about comprehending how and why your authenticity serves as a powerful catalyst in this process. Every interaction with a potential client is an opportunity to solidify their trust in you, which is the cornerstone of any purchasing decision. Trust is built not merely through the promises we make but, significantly, through the ones we consistently fulfil. This integrity, a fundamental aspect of our authentic storytelling approach, reassures clients that they are making the right choice, an essential factor in a landscape crowded with options and claims.

Trust is deeply intertwined with another critical psychological aspect: authenticity. In today's market, consumers are increasingly savvy and sceptical of traditional sales tactics that feel impersonal or disingenuous. They seek connections that are real and brands that not only understand their needs but reflect their values and aspirations. This is where our authentic content creation becomes a strategic asset. By sharing real stories, genuine emotions and true outcomes, we do more than capture interest; we create an emotional resonance that can profoundly influence buyer behaviour.

In an era where the digital marketplace is more saturated than ever, traditional 'bro' marketing techniques – characterised by aggressive tactics and hyperbolic claims – are increasingly ineffective. Today's discerning consumers seek genuine connections and authenticity, compelling brands to rethink their approach to sales copy. As we navigate the crowded world of online business, the true challenges and opportunities lie in how we articulate our experiences and values. It is not just about choosing the right words but, as we've already discussed, about weaving stories and evoking emotions that resonate deeply, aligning with our audience's aspirations and challenges.

Effective sales copy today does more than enumerate features and benefits; it should mirror the brand's core values and resonate on an emotional level, making each potential client feel seen, understood and genuinely valued. This deeper connection is achieved not through manipulation but by empowering the reader. A truly impactful sales message enables potential buyers to perceive the offerings as directly relevant to their lives or businesses, whether by solving a pressing problem or enhancing their daily reality. This level of relevance is cultivated through a nuanced understanding of not just demographic but psychographic details: the motivations, fears, desires and values that drive consumer behaviour.

In this dynamic digital age, leveraging the psychological triggers of reciprocity, scarcity, authority, commitment and consistency can significantly enhance your sales strategies. However, these triggers must be applied ethically and authentically to avoid the pitfalls of traditional sales tactics that can alienate modern consumers. For example, the principle of scarcity – often used to hurry consumers with limited-time offers – should be employed in a way that respects the intelligence of your audience, perhaps by emphasising the genuine exclusivity of an offer due to the bespoke nature of a product or service.

Similarly, the authority principle should be based on true expertise and shared in a way that educates and informs rather than dictates. Showcasing testimonials, detailed case studies and thought leadership can help establish credibility and build trust without resorting to overt or aggressive sales pitches.

Commitment and consistency are about reinforcing the potential client's journey with your brand, ensuring that each interaction they have reinforces their decision to trust you. This could be through consistent messaging that echoes across various platforms or follow-up communications that reaffirm your brand's commitment to their satisfaction and success.

As we take a deeper look at these psychological triggers, we'll explore how they can be weaved into your sales copy to not only boost conversions but deepen the trust and loyalty of your client base. By understanding and employing these principles thoughtfully, you align what your brand offers with what your clients need, transforming casual browsers into committed buyers and one-time clients into loyal, long-term advocates.

By the end of this section, you will be better equipped to use the power of psychological sales techniques within the framework of authentic storytelling. Your sales copy will then not merely be a tool for conversion, but a continuation of the meaningful dialogue you've established with your audience, inviting them into an ongoing relationship where your offerings resonate as necessary, valued and uniquely tailored to their needs. This approach doesn't just sell a product or service; it affirms the ongoing value of the relationship you've built, making your audience eager not only to buy but to continue the conversation and deepen their engagement with your brand.

Crafting a sales narrative that connects and converts

When it comes to selling, fearlessness plays a crucial role. As we already discussed earlier on, it's not the absence of fear but the courage to act despite it. This bravery is especially pivotal when integrating your authentic brand story into your sales narrative. To sell fearlessly, you must believe wholeheartedly in the value of what you offer and communicate this conviction through stories that not only engage but resonate deeply with your audience. Here is how you do that in four simple steps:

1. Make sure you have a detailed understanding of your clients' needs

For solo entrepreneurs or small business owners, the intimate understanding of your clients' needs is a powerful tool. Begin by meticulously researching and empathising with the challenges your clients face. This could involve conducting surveys, market research calls or monitoring discussions on social media platforms relevant to your industry. This deep dive will not only enhance your understanding but enable you to write sales copy that feels like a direct conversation with each potential client.

For instance, if you're a freelance graphic designer, your target clients might struggle with creating visually compelling content that captures their brand's essence. In your sales copy, explicitly acknowledge these challenges and detail how your design solutions have helped similar businesses enhance their visual branding. Use specific, relatable examples and before-and-after scenarios to paint a vivid picture of the potential transformations you offer.

2. Weaving authenticity into every message

Authenticity in your messaging means sharing the raw, real stories behind your brand. It is about transparency and vulnerability, showcasing the highs and the trials that have shaped your business journey. Reflect this authenticity in your sales copy by sharing your philosophy, your approach to business and the core values that drive your decisions.

For example, if you run an online coaching business, you might share your own transformation story - how overcoming certain personal obstacles inspired you to help others. Detail the specific methods you used, the challenges you faced and how this journey informs your coaching practices today. This not only humanises your brand but strengthens the emotional impact of your sales copy, making it compelling and relatable.

3. Aligning your narrative with client aspirations

Your sales copy should seamlessly connect your offerings to the dreams and aspirations of your audience. This alignment is crucial not just for answering the immediate needs, but for inspiring your clients to see the bigger picture of what they could achieve with your help.

If you sell digital courses on financial management, for example, don't just list the course contents. Instead, include narratives around how mastering budgeting and investment strategies can lead to financial freedom and the ability to pursue personal passions. Use language that evokes emotion and paints a picture of the lifestyle benefits that come from using your products or services.

4. Showcasing detailed success stories and heartfelt testimonials

Nothing builds trust and breaks down scepticism like detailed success stories and genuine testimonials. However, instead of simply listing testimonials, integrate them into a narrative format that tells a compelling story. Discuss the client's initial challenges, the process of working with you, the solutions implemented and the outcomes achieved.

For example, if you provide digital marketing services, describe a client's journey from low online engagement to a thriving community of followers and clients. Include specific metrics, such as growth percentages and revenue increases, to substantiate your claims. Make these stories relatable by focusing on the client's initial scepticism and their journey to seeing tangible results.

By embedding these detailed and authentic elements into your sales copy, you transform it from mere promotional text to a compelling part of your ongoing conversation with your audience. This approach not only enhances the persuasiveness of your copy but reaffirms the trust and commitment that are essential in the digital age's competitive marketplace. Your sales narrative becomes a powerful extension of your brand story, engaging your audience on a deeper level and motivating them to take action.

Mastering the craft of writing sales copy that resonates and converts is not an overnight achievement; it requires consistent practice and a fearless commitment to understanding and speaking to your ideal client's deepest needs and desires. As you implement the strategies discussed - deeply understanding client needs, weaving authenticity into every message, aligning with client aspirations and showcasing success stories - you'll develop a more intuitive and effective approach to your sales narrative. However, becoming truly adept at this requires regular reflection and adaptation. Each piece of sales copy you create is an opportunity to refine your skills, test new approaches and learn more about what resonates with your audience.

Remember, fearlessness in sales comes from a profound, deep-rooted belief in the value of what you offer. It is about more than just overcoming the initial hesitation to ask for the sale; it is about embracing the confidence that what you are providing can and will genuinely make a difference in your clients' lives. With each sales pitch, you're not just seeking a transaction; you are inviting your audience into a transformative experience.

This ongoing practice not only sharpens your skills but deepens your understanding of your market, allowing you to write copy that hits the mark more consistently. As you continue to iterate and engage with your clients, your authenticity will shine through not just as a marketer, but as a trusted advisor whose offerings are integral to their success. So while the path to becoming a fearless sales copywriter may be challenging, it is also immensely rewarding. Keep at it, believe in your value and let your genuine passion for your work guide you. With commitment and practice, you will find that writing compelling, conversion-oriented sales copy becomes a natural extension of your authentic brand story, driving not only sales but lasting client relationships.

The art of the offer

Your offer is not just a statement of what you provide; it is a declaration of the unique value you bring to your clients' lives or businesses. Crafting this message requires a deep understanding of copywriting techniques that highlight your offerings' uniqueness and value, ensuring that your audience perceives them as not just another option, but the only choice that truly meets their needs.

You need to begin by ensuring your offer is crystal clear. Your audience should understand exactly what you are offering and how it benefits them without having to sift through jargon or overly complex descriptions. The simplicity of your message can significantly enhance its effectiveness, as it allows potential clients to quickly grasp the value of your product or service. For instance, if you are a web developer offering custom website solutions, your offer should clearly state how your service helps businesses enhance their online presence and attract more clients, emphasising ease of use and bespoke design that aligns perfectly with their brand identity.

Next, focus on differentiating your offer from the competition. This involves a keen understanding of your unique selling proposition and communicating it compellingly through your sales copy. Describe not only what you offer but why it is superior or different from what is already out there. For a tech consultant, this might involve emphasising a unique methodology that has consistently yielded impressive results for clients, or exclusive access to industry insights that others do not provide. Use specific examples and data to back up your claims, making your offer not only attractive but credible.

Your sales copy should always emphasise the value your clients will receive from choosing your product or service. This goes beyond listing features or services; it involves painting a picture of the positive changes that will occur as a result of their purchase. For example, if you offer a personal fitness programme, do not just talk about the programme components; focus on the outcomes: increased energy, better health metrics and a transformed body image. Use emotive language to connect these outcomes to your client's deepest desires and goals, making the benefits tangible and desirable.

Finally, when it comes time to make your offer, do it with unwavering confidence and conviction. This confidence stems from a genuine belief in the transformative power of what you are selling and a deep understanding of its alignment with your clients' needs. Position your offer not as a mere choice among many, but as the definitive solution to their problem. Communicate a sense of urgency and necessity, but do so authentically – let your enthusiasm for their success and your role in that journey shine through every word.

The call to action (CTA) is the crescendo of your sales pitch, the point where interest is meant to transform into action. To be effective, a CTA must be direct, clear and compelling. It should spur your audience to act decisively, whether it's "Book your free consultation today," "Join now by clicking the link below and transform your life," or "Fill in the contact box to start your journey towards success with us." Each of these examples is designed to leave potential clients feeling excited and ready to take the next step. They know exactly what to do and how to do it, which respects their time and simplifies their decision-making process.

Talking specifically about social media, a passive CTA like "DM me for more details" often fails to achieve the desired impact. This approach places the burden of action on the potential client, a risky move considering the rapid pace at which users scroll through their feeds. If the CTA doesn't grab their attention and make it incredibly easy to act, you risk losing them. A more effective CTA is direct and reduces friction, telling people precisely what they will get and how to get it, such as "Click on the link below to sign up now," or "Download this instantly by entering your email - link below." This method makes the journey to obtain your product or service as seamless as possible, not merely gauging interest but facilitating the decision-making process.

However, it's important to recognise exceptions, particularly with high-ticket items like an exclusive coaching package, for example. In these instances where the investment is significant, a CTA inviting potential clients to "DM for more details" can be appropriate, as it adds an element of exclusivity and personal connection that high-value offers often require. The key is in how you frame this invitation. Rather than a generic "DM for more details," add a sense of urgency and exclusivity: "I'm offering a limited number of spots for this opportunity. DM me to see if you qualify." This creates scarcity, enhancing the perceived value of the offer. Of course, make sure that the scarcity, if you choose to use it, is genuine.

Alternatively, for a more personalised approach, you might use: "Serious about achieving [result your offer promises]? Let's talk. DM me for a private consultation about [your offer]." This signals a tailored, one-on-one interaction, appealing directly to those who are serious about a high-level service. Or, for a more engaging twist: “Think you’ve got what it takes to join [your programme]? I am looking for [specific number/type of people] ready to achieve [desired outcome]. DM me to find out if you’re one of them!” This not only challenges but excites the reader, effectively calling the right type of person into action.

While “DM for more details” can sometimes appear lazy and generally less effective for standard offers, when crafted with thoughtfulness and strategic intent, it can serve as a powerful tool for engaging potential clients in high-ticket sales. Remember, the effectiveness of your CTA lies not just in what it says but in how well it aligns with the nature of the offer and the expectations of your audience. By carefully designing your CTAs, you ensure that each one is not merely a directive but an integral part of a compelling sales narrative that drives action and deepens engagement with your brand.

By combining clarity, uniqueness, value orientation and confident presentation, your offers will not just capture attention; they will convert prospects into loyal clients. Each element of your offer builds upon the last, creating a comprehensive and compelling narrative that speaks directly to the needs and desires of your audience. This approach does not just sell a product or a service; it sells an experience and a result that is too valuable to pass up. Thus, your offers become not just one of many options, but the essential choice for anyone seeking solutions you provide.

Persuasive techniques for sales copy

As we transition deeper into the mechanics of conversion in sales, it becomes essential to learn how to use the subtle art of persuasion in your copywriting. This isn't about coercing a sale, but about artfully crafting messages that resonate on a deeper psychological level, compelling your audience to act not out of pressure, but because they feel genuinely connected and understood. Here, we're going to explore how to ethically employ persuasive techniques in your sales copy, ensuring your messages are both effective and true to the spirit of authentic engagement.

The power of language in persuasion cannot be overstated. The words you choose can stir emotions, shift perspectives and motivate action. Let's dissect how you can leverage key psychological triggers such as scarcity, urgency and exclusivity to enhance the appeal of your offerings:

1. Scarcity: creating value through limitation

Scarcity is a powerful psychological trigger because it capitalises on humans' innate fear of missing out (otherwise known as 'FOMO'). When something is scarce, it's perceived as more valuable, making it more desirable. This principle can be effectively applied to your sales strategies to boost engagement and urgency.

For example, imagine you are launching a coaching programme designed to offer intense, personalised guidance to ensure significant personal or professional growth. Limiting availability to just ten spots not only ensures you can deliver on your promise of personal connection but significantly raises the perceived value of your programme. Your sales copy might say: "Secure your place in this exclusive coaching programme - only ten spots available to guarantee personalised attention and transformative results." This message does more than inform; it emphasises the uniqueness of the opportunity and creates a sense of urgency that compels the audience to act quickly to avoid missing out.

2. Urgency: motivating immediate action

Urgency is a tactic that encourages people to act quickly, often leveraging time-sensitive incentives. It is particularly effective when you've already established value and trust with your audience, and it can be the nudge that converts interest into decisive action.

Consider offering a limited-time discount on a popular course, such as a digital marketing bootcamp that has had rave reviews and proven results. By introducing a 24-hour discount, your copy could effectively push those on the fence to commit. Phrases like "Act now - save 30% on our acclaimed digital marketing bootcamp, offer expires in 24 hours!" can create a compelling call to action. This not only communicates the benefit of acting quickly (the discount) but plays on the natural human tendency to avoid regrets associated with missing out.

3. Exclusivity: aligning with aspirations

Exclusivity elevates an offer by making it seem specially tailored for a specific audience, enhancing its attractiveness. This approach works exceptionally well when you can align the exclusivity of your offer with the aspirations or identity of your target market.

If you're targeting small business owners with a marketing masterclass designed to scale their operations, for example, exclusivity can be a strong selling point. Your sales copy might frame the masterclass as an elite programme, available only to those who are truly committed to achieving substantial growth. For instance: "Join my exclusive masterclass, tailored for driven entrepreneurs ready to catapult their business to multi-six figures. Limited seats available to maintain an intimate, high-impact learning environment." This language not only stresses the unique nature of the offer but matches the ambition level of the target audience, making it highly appealing.

Ethical use of persuasive techniques

Incorporating psychological triggers like scarcity, urgency and exclusivity in your sales copy can significantly enhance the appeal of your offerings. However, the ethical application of these techniques is not just a 'best practice'; it is essential for maintaining trust and integrity with your audience. Misusing these triggers can quickly backfire, leading to consumer scepticism and damage to your brand's reputation.

When you claim an offer is scarce, time-sensitive or exclusive, your audience must find these claims credible. Today's consumers are exceptionally discerning; they can often sense when a sales tactic is contrived. People talk, and in an age dominated by social media and online reviews, one false move can be widely publicised, quickly tarnishing your brand's image. For example, if clients notice that your 'last chance' offer is still available weeks later, or if a 'limited edition' product continually restocks, the illusion of scarcity and urgency shatters.

Writing copy that falsely employs these triggers not only risks public exposure but sends a subtext of desperation or deceit. When a business frequently pushes supposedly limited-time deals or exclusive offers that aren't genuinely limited, it suggests a lack of confidence in the products or services' inherent value. This incongruence between what is said and what is perceived can erode trust as savvy clients read between the lines, sensing the disparity between the message and the reality.

To use scarcity, urgency and exclusivity responsibly and effectively, every claim you make must be backed by truth. If you promote a product as available only for a limited time, ensure the deadline is real. If you offer a product with limited stock, the quantity should truly be limited. This transparency is crucial – it validates the trust your clients and followers place in your brand and reaffirms your commitment to ethical business practices.

For instance, if you're offering signed copies of a book and claim that only fifty are available, those fifty should be the only ones in existence. Fulfilling this promise not only satisfies those who make a purchase but enhances your reputation among those who might consider future offers.

By integrating these psychological triggers into your sales strategy authentically, you align your marketing efforts with the foundational principles of your brand. This alignment transforms your sales copy from mere promotional text to a sincere extension of the relationship you've built with your audience. It is about enriching these connections with honesty and integrity, creating not just transactions but lasting engagements based on mutual respect and trust.

This approach not only respects your audience's intelligence but enhances their overall experience with your brand, causing both immediate sales and later building long-term loyalty. When you handle these powerful psychological triggers with care and respect, they don't just serve your sales objectives; they reinforce the authenticity and ethical stance that are core to your brand's message, deeply resonating in today's marketplace where honesty is both appreciated and expected.

NLP techniques for ethical persuasion

Neuro-linguistic programming (NLP) represents a fascinating convergence of linguistics, psychology and behavioural science. Developed in the 1970s by Richard Bandler and John Grinder, it originated from their curiosity about the patterns behind exceptional success. NLP is grounded in the idea that by deciphering and emulating the language structures and behavioural patterns of highly successful individuals, anyone can enhance their effectiveness and achieve their goals.

In essence, NLP explores the relationships between how we think (neuro), how we communicate (linguistic) and our patterns of behaviour and emotion (programming). It posits that these can be altered to achieve specific goals in life. By studying and modelling the cognitive behaviours of those who excel in certain fields, NLP aims to synthesise the processes behind their successes into a replicable form that others can follow to improve their own performance in various aspects of life.

NLP is lauded for its potential applications across various domains, from improving personal interactions and enhancing communication skills to overcoming mental barriers and achieving greater career success. For instance, a sales professional might use NLP techniques to better understand and mirror the communication style of potential clients, thereby building rapport and trust more effectively. Meanwhile, therapists might employ NLP to help clients reframe traumatic memories, reducing their emotional impact and aiding healing.

When it comes to copywriting, NLP can be an invaluable tool to enhance the persuasive power of text. It is particularly effective in marketing and sales strategies, where the subtle influence of language can significantly impact consumer behaviour. However, despite its potential benefits, NLP is not without controversy. One common misconception is that NLP is a form of mental manipulation. This stems from techniques such as 'mirroring' and 'anchoring', which can be misinterpreted as methods for covertly influencing others. However, when applied ethically, these techniques are used to help the potential client understand and connect with you, not to control or deceive them.

Traditionally, NLP has been used in therapy, coaching and personal development settings. Therapists might use NLP to help clients change negative thought patterns and behaviours, while coaches use it to assist people in achieving personal and professional goals. For instance, a therapist might help a client who is afraid of public speaking by changing the submodalities (the qualities of how they internally represent their fear), such as adjusting the mental images, sounds or feelings associated with the fear to make it less intense.

Building on its traditional applications in therapeutic and coaching environments, NLP offers equally transformative potential for enhancing communication in other domains, including marketing and copywriting. In these contexts, the principles of NLP can be ingeniously adapted to craft messages that resonate on a deeper psychological level, thus developing stronger and more meaningful connections with an audience. Here is how

NLP can be integrated into copywriting to connect more profoundly with an audience:

1. Mirroring language

Mirroring language is a cornerstone NLP technique that involves adapting your language to reflect the tone, style and vocabulary of your target audience. This alignment creates a sense of familiarity and trust, making your message feel more personal and relatable. For example, if you're targeting tech enthusiasts, incorporating specific jargon like 'augmented reality' or 'machine learning' can make your content resonate. Conversely, for a health and wellness audience, using calm, nurturing language and terms like 'holistic', 'wellbeing' and 'mindfulness' can enhance relatability. By mirroring the linguistic preferences of your audience, you subtly affirm that your brand understands and speaks their language.

2. Anchoring

Anchoring is an influential NLP tactic that involves connecting an emotional response with a specific action or stimulus. In copywriting, you can utilise this by associating positive emotions with your product or service. For instance, a luxury car brand might use language that evokes feelings of prestige and success, such as: "Take the driver's seat in a realm of unparalleled luxury and power - experience driving as it should be". Here, the act of driving the car is anchored to feelings of success and exclusivity, making the prospect of purchasing the car more appealing.

3. Commanding language

Using commanding language effectively means embedding subtle commands within your narrative that guide the reader towards envisaging positive outcomes and taking action. This technique should be woven into the narrative subtly to avoid overt directives that might be off-putting. For example, an estate agent might use phrases like "imagine waking up to breathtaking ocean views from your new home". This not only encourages potential buyers to visualise living in the property but connects emotionally, making the idea more attractive and tangible.

4. Reframing

Reframing in copywriting means presenting a product or situation in a way that shifts the reader's perspective, often transforming perceived weaknesses into strengths. This technique can be particularly useful in addressing objections or enhancing perceived value. For instance, if a service requires a substantial upfront investment, the copy might reframe this by emphasising the exceptional return on investment (ROI) and long-term savings, thus shifting the narrative from 'expensive' to 'valuable'. An example could be: "Investing in this premium software isn't a cost; it is an investment in streamlining your operations and boosting efficiency that pays dividends in the long run."

It is important to note that it's absolutely crucial to apply NLP techniques ethically. This means using NLP to enhance understanding and connection rather than manipulation. Transparency should be at the heart of any communication. Ensuring that the emotional responses elicited are genuine and that the actions you're encouraging are in the best interests of the audience respects both the power of NLP and the autonomy of your readers.

Incorporating NLP into copywriting, when aligned with the theme of authenticity from our earlier discussions, transforms not just the style but the substance of your communication. It is about using NLP to deepen the connection between your brand and your audience, making your messages not only more persuasive but more meaningful and aligned with the values and needs of your audience. By practising these techniques regularly and reflecting upon their impact, you can refine your approach to ensure that your sales copy not only drives conversions but builds lasting relationships based on trust and genuine engagement. This is the essence of using persuasion ethically in business: it's not just about selling products but about creating meaningful exchanges that enrich both the provider and the consumer, creating a community around shared values and mutual benefit.

In practice, the careful, mindful application of NLP in your sales copy should be seen as an extension of your brand's commitment to authenticity. It should reflect a genuine understanding and respect for your audience, contributing to a marketing strategy that values long-term relationships over short-term gains. This is how you transform the art of selling into an authentic dialogue between your brand and your clients, creating not only immediate sales success but sustainable business growth.

The act of selling is not a departure from the art of communication, but a continuation

As we conclude this chapter on mastering the art of the sale, it's essential to reflect upon the profound connection between the stories we tell and the responses they invoke. The techniques we've explored - from understanding the psychology of sales to implementing Neuro-linguistic programming - are not just tools to enhance conversion rates; they are extensions of a narrative that starts with genuine engagement and culminates in an invitation to participate in something greater.

Fearlessness in asking for the sale comes from a deep belief in the value of what you offer. It is rooted in the authenticity of your message and the integrity of your approach. Each strategy discussed, from leveraging scarcity and urgency to employing NLP techniques like mirroring language and anchoring emotions, should be seen not as tactics to manipulate, but as methods to communicate more effectively and connect more deeply.

Remember, the act of selling is not a departure from the art of connection; it is a continuation. When done right, it's a powerful affirmation of everything your brand stands for. You are not just closing a deal and adding more cash to your bottom line; you are inviting your audience to join you in a shared vision, to partake in a solution that you genuinely believe will enhance their lives or businesses. This is where the courage to ask for the sale stems from. It is really all about embracing the confidence that your product or service is not just a choice, but the choice that will make a real difference.

Let this chapter serve not only as a guide to refining your sales techniques, but as a manifesto for courageously genuine engagement in every aspect of your business dealings. The strategies laid out are your tools to not only meet business objectives but to enrich the relationships you cherish with your clients. When you approach each sales interaction from a place of authenticity, backed by a solid understanding of your audience's needs and desires, you transform the sales process into an enriching experience that benefits both parties.

As you move forward, practise these techniques with the awareness that true mastery comes from continuous application and refinement. Each client interaction, each sales pitch and every piece of marketing copy is an opportunity to hone your skills, learn more about what resonates with your audience and further align your offerings with their aspirations.

Embrace this journey with an open heart and a fearless spirit. Trust in the value of your offerings and the authenticity of your narrative. Let these be the guiding forces that drive your sales strategy. With each step forward, reinforce the trust your clients place in you by consistently delivering on your promises and continuously demonstrating your commitment to their success.

In the end, selling fearlessly isn't just about being bold enough to ask for the sale; it is about being confident enough to know that what you're offering is not just a product or service, but a gateway to a better outcome - a shared success story. This conviction, paired with the techniques and insights you've gained, will not only increase your sales but transform how you connect with every person your business touches.

Now, armed with these tools and empowered by a deeper understanding of the ethical application of persuasive techniques, step forward into each sales dialogue not as a transaction, but as a meaningful exchange. Turn your fear of asking for the sale into the courage to offer an opportunity. Remember, each time you do, you're not just selling; you are enriching lives and businesses.

7
Desire and Deliverance

As we journey deeper into the art of fearless words, this chapter introduces a pivotal concept in marketing and sales: aligning what potential clients think they want with what they truly need. This alignment goes beyond transactional exchanges; it is about understanding and responding to the underlying motivations that drive consumer behaviour.

Often, consumers are driven by immediate desires, shaped by trends, advertising and peer influences. They come to us with a preconceived notion of what they want, which might not always align with what would serve them best in the long term. For instance, you may desire the latest smartphone model because of its popularity or new features advertised heavily in the media. However, what you might actually need is a reliable, user-friendly phone that meets your daily requirements without unnecessary complexity or cost.

Our challenge, and indeed our responsibility, is to navigate these waters with integrity. This involves not just selling to potential clients but engaging with them educatively, helping them bridge the gap between fleeting wants and enduring needs. This approach does not dilute the essence of what they seek; rather, it enhances their understanding and appreciation of what they truly require. By doing so, we ensure that our marketing and sales strategies are not only effective but deeply respectful and genuinely helpful.

When it comes to our content writing and copywriting, this concept takes a unique shape. We are tasked with crafting messages that resonate on both emotional and practical levels. Our words must tap into the initial desires that draw our audience towards a product or service, while subtly guiding them towards a deeper recognition of their needs. This is where the craft of fearless words comes into play to not just persuade, but enlighten and transform the consumer's understanding.

For example, consider a scenario where you're marketing a high-end yoga retreat in Bali. The initial desire of potential clients might be driven by the allure of an exotic location or the promise of relaxation. While these are valid wants, what they might truly need is a deeper, transformative experience that addresses stress management and personal growth. Your copy needs to seduce with the immediate benefits but also educate about the deeper value, connecting their initial desire for relaxation with a comprehensive programme that offers lasting wellness benefits.

By the end of this chapter, you should be equipped not only with the understanding of how to align consumer wants with their actual needs, but with the skills to implement these strategies in your writing. The goal is to ensure that your content does more than capture attention; it should educate, inspire and lead to more informed, satisfied clients. This approach not only builds trust and loyalty but elevates your brand as a thought leader who values the wellbeing and satisfaction of its audience.

What compels us to desire?

Diving into the roots of consumer desires is akin to peeling back the layers of an onion. Each layer reveals motivations and drives that shape our decisions, often without our conscious awareness. During our journey to connect wants with needs through fearless and articulate words, understanding these underlying forces becomes paramount.

So what compels a person to desire a particular product or service? On the surface, it may appear to be a straightforward question, but the answers are as varied and complex as human nature itself. Some are drawn to the shimmering allure of status, seeking products that signal a certain socioeconomic standing to their peers. For these consumers, a luxury car or high-end fashion brand does more than serve a functional purpose; it communicates wealth, taste and a sense of belonging to an exclusive group.

Others might be driven by a search for comfort or health benefits, where products are not just purchased but chosen for the promise of a better life. Consider the rise in popularity of ergonomic office furniture designed to alleviate back pain or high-performance blenders promoted to utilise the nutritional benefits of whole foods. These aren't just basic purchases; they are investments in personal wellbeing.

Then there are those motivated by fear or aspiration, which often go hand in hand. The fear of missing out (FOMO) can drive the need to buy the latest gadget, not out of a genuine need for the product, but out of an anxiety to keep up with technological trends. Conversely, aspiration pushes individuals to acquire goods that symbolise the life they yearn for, be it a set of professional-grade kitchen knives for the aspiring chef or a sophisticated DSLR camera for the budding photographer.

Understanding these motivations requires us to not only listen but engage deeply with the narratives that our clients live by and the identities they aspire to manifest. As marketers, our task is to weave these understandings into our narratives, making our words a bridge that connects product features with human emotions and desires. In the craft of fearless words, we use our insights to mould messages that resonate deeply not just with the surface desires, but with the core needs of our audience. This is where the magic of effective copywriting lies – it is about tapping into that deeper vein of human experience and aspiration, making the connection between what people think they want and what they truly need.

When we write a piece of content, whether it's a blog post, a web page or a social media post, we're not just presenting a product or service; we are offering a narrative that aligns with the personal stories of our audience. This narrative doesn't coerce. Instead, it enlightens and guides. It shows how a product doesn't just add to a pile of possessions but enriches lives in meaningful ways.

For instance, consider a marketing campaign for a sustainable clothing brand. The immediate consumer desire might be to follow a trend towards eco-friendly products. However, their deeper need could be to contribute positively to the environment and feel good about their consumer choices. Here, the copy doesn't just sell clothes; it sells a commitment to sustainability and an invitation to be part of a larger movement. It educates the consumer about the environmental impact of fast fashion, thus aligning their initial desire for trendy clothing with a more profound commitment to planetary health.

This approach is grounded in the ethical use of persuasive techniques. By understanding the psychological drivers behind consumer behaviour – whether it's seeking status, comfort, health or fulfilling aspirations – we tailor our messages to resonate on a deeper level. This doesn't just enhance the effectiveness of our content; it builds trust and credibility. Consumers feel understood and respected, not manipulated, which builds long-term relationships and loyalty.

Incorporating these insights into our writing requires not only a keen understanding of psychology, but a masterful command of language. We need to craft sentences that breathe life into the features of a product or service, turning them into benefits that echo the innermost desires and needs of our audience. This is the art of transformational copywriting, where features are not simply listed out, but presented as gateways to achieving personal aspirations or solving real problems.

Building on our understanding of consumer motivations, we next turn our attention to refining how we communicate that deeper understanding back to our audience. The delicate task ahead involves educating our potential clients about what they truly need in a way that respects their initial desires without belittling them. This is not simply about correcting misconceptions or directing choices; it is about empowering consumers with knowledge and insight, thus enhancing their decision-making processes.

Educational engagement requires a nuanced approach in content writing and creation. We are tasked with creating narratives that are informative yet engaging, authoritative yet approachable. It is about striking a balance where information delivery becomes as compelling as storytelling. This transformation of facts into narratives involves a high level of skill in content writing and copywriting, where every word and phrase is chosen not just for its direct meaning, but for its power to connect and resonate.

For example, imagine you are writing content for a dietary supplement designed to enhance cognitive function. The consumer might initially be drawn to the product by a desire to improve memory based on a simple benefit touted in an advertisement. Our job as fearless communicators is to build upon this initial interest by educating the consumer about the holistic benefits of cognitive health, such as improved mood, better problem-solving abilities and long-term neuro-protective effects. The content should not just sell a supplement; it should offer a gateway to a healthier, more vibrant life. Here, the educational content can include data-driven blog posts, engaging infographics that break down the science behind cognitive health and case studies that weave real stories with factual information, making the educational journey personal and relatable.

This educational approach also involves a clear understanding of the language and metaphors that resonate with our target audience. Here, we employ a style of writing that mirrors the readers' level of understanding and expands upon it. This means using analogies that are within their grasp, introducing complex ideas gradually and connecting these ideas back to the common things we experience in our everyday life. It is about making the unknown known and the unfamiliar familiar.

Deepening our understanding of educational engagement requires a thoughtful approach to language and communication styles that are tailored specifically to our audience's experiences and expectations. In writing content that educates without alienating, the choice of language, the metaphors used and the complexity of information presented must all be carefully calibrated to meet the reader where they are and guide them towards deeper insights.

Let's consider a practical example of this approach in action. Suppose we are developing content for a financial services company that aims to introduce consumers to the concept of investment portfolios. The target audience is professionals aged 30-40 who have a basic understanding of savings but are novices in investments. To bridge this gap, the language used must demystify the complexities of financial instruments without oversimplifying the strategic importance of investment decisions.

For example, instead of starting with technical jargon like 'diversified portfolios' and 'asset allocation', we might begin with a relatable analogy: "Think of building an investment portfolio like planting a garden. Just as you would plant a mix of flowers, fruits and vegetables to ensure something blooms or ripens through each season, diversifying your investments ensures that different parts of your financial garden will thrive under different economic conditions."

This analogy does more than simplify; it connects the concept of investment to everyday activities familiar to the target audience, making the unfamiliar concept of investment portfolios more approachable and understandable. By gradually introducing more complex ideas, such as the types of investments that might correspond to different plants in their garden (stocks as flowers for quick growth, bonds as vegetables for steady produce), we can expand the reader's understanding in a structured, relatable way.

Continuing with this narrative, the content could then delve deeper into specifics: "After planting your garden, you need to manage it: watering, pruning and sometimes adding fertiliser. Similarly, managing an investment portfolio involves reviewing and adjusting your assets to align with your growth goals and risk tolerance, just like how some plants need more sunlight or water than others."

By breaking down complex financial advice into steps analogous to a generally well-understood topic like gardening, the content remains accessible. Each piece builds on the last, reinforcing knowledge and confidence. This method not only educates but empowers the reader by relating new financial concepts to a well-understood framework.

When content resonates in a language that feels familiar, it does more than inform; it engages and transforms the reader's understanding. This approach not only makes the educational content more digestible but strengthens the connection between the brand and its audience, leading to a deeper, more meaningful relationship.

Moreover, educational engagement through copywriting should aim to empower. Instead of merely instructing, our words should encourage exploration, question-asking and further research. We create content that invites interaction, whether through calls to action that encourage readers to download a lead magnet, sign up for a webinar or participate in community discussions. Each piece of content should feel like an invitation to a broader conversation, not a conclusion.

Let's take a look at a detailed example of how this can be implemented through the promotion of a webinar on sustainable living practices. The target audience is environmentally conscious consumers who are already aware of basic recycling and conservation practices but may not understand more complex sustainability issues like zero-waste lifestyles or the impact of fast fashion.

So imagine you are creating a series of blog posts for a nonprofit organisation focused on environmental advocacy. The series aims to promote an upcoming webinar titled: "Beyond Recycling: Everyday Actions for a Sustainable Future." The objective is to deepen the audience's understanding of sustainability and to motivate them to adopt more impactful environmental practices.

Your blog post structure might look something like this:

1. Introduction

Begin with a compelling fact that highlights a common misconception about recycling, such as: "While recycling is crucial, it addresses only a small fraction of global waste. What if you could do more every day to help the planet?" This opening sets the stage for challenging the reader's existing knowledge and piquing their interest in discovering more comprehensive solutions.

2. Body

Introduce the concept of zero-waste lifestyles with simple explanations and real-life examples. For instance: “Imagine if nothing from your morning routine ended up in a landfill. Your toothbrush? Bamboo. Your shampoo? Refilled at the local Co-op. It is not just possible; it is practical.” You could then use interactive elements like quizzes within the post to assess the reader’s current practices, such as: “How many items in your daily routine could be swapped for sustainable alternatives? Take the quiz to find out!” Encourage the reader to reflect upon their personal impact and the broader implications of their choices, leading to a deeper personal connection to the topic.

3. Conclusion

End with a strong call to action that links directly to the registration page for the webinar. For example: “Ready to transform your environmental impact? Join the free webinar to explore practical steps towards a sustainable lifestyle. Register now by clicking the link below and start your journey to zero waste.” Include an invitation to join a community discussion group on social media where participants can share their experiences, challenges and successes in implementing sustainable practices. This community aspect helps to build a network of support and continuous learning.

In this example, the content does more than simply inform the reader about sustainability; it challenges them to evaluate their current practices, introduces them to accessible alternatives and invites them to learn more through a webinar. The interactive quiz acts as both an educational tool and a lead magnet, drawing the reader deeper into the topic while capturing their contact information for further engagement. The community discussion group facilitates ongoing dialogue, making each participant feel they are part of a larger movement towards change.

As we continue to thread our audience through the narrative from what they want to what they need, our tone plays a crucial role. It must be empathetic and respectful, never condescending. We acknowledge the validity of their initial desires and frame our educational content as a value-add, not a correction. We are here not to dictate but to guide, not to dismiss but to offer something more: a deeper understanding and perhaps a solution that they hadn't considered. By mastering educational engagement, we not only end up with a better-informed consumer base but build trust and credibility. Our audience learns to see us not just as sellers, but as allies in their journey towards making choices that truly enrich their lives. This relationship, founded on respect and empowerment, is the essence of what it means to write with fearless words in the world of marketing and sales.

Ethical persuasion in copywriting

Building on the foundation of educational engagement, we pivot to the crucial theme of ethical persuasion, the backbone of our approach in connecting with our audience. When it comes to copywriting, the line between persuasion and manipulation can be thin, but it's a boundary we must respect meticulously. The essence of ethical persuasion lies in respecting the intelligence and autonomy of our audience, guiding them through meticulously crafted messages that create genuine understanding and encourage informed decisions.

Persuasive writing, when executed ethically, serves as a powerful tool that extends beyond just conversions; it educates, enlightens and aligns with the deeper needs and aspirations of the audience. This approach demands a deep understanding of the ethical implications of our words, ensuring that we're not merely seducing the audience into making a purchase but genuinely assisting them in realising how our offerings can enrich their lives.

When it comes to conversion copywriting, ethical persuasion is crucial for building long-term success and maintaining trust with your clients. This brings us to transparency: the cornerstone of trust, which is particularly vital for businesses whose services might seem intangible. Take the example of an online business coach. Instead of vaguely promising to "Transform your life in weeks," it's more forthright and practical to specify what the coaching sessions will cover, such as: "Develop targeted strategies to enhance your leadership skills over twelve sessions." This clarity not only manages expectations but builds credibility, showcasing a commitment to honesty over making exaggerated claims.

Moving to informed consent, it's essential for clients to fully understand what they are signing up for, including all the terms and conditions of the service. If you run a subscription-based service or membership, for example, ensure that clients are fully aware of what the subscription includes, how they can benefit from it and the terms of cancellation. Providing a detailed FAQ on your signup page or explicit footnotes under subscription options that outline renewal policies and cancellation procedures can make all the difference. Such transparency ensures that clients feel well-informed and secure in their decisions, bolstering their trust in your business.

When it comes to using emotional appeal, it's important to inspire and motivate without manipulating. For instance, if you offer digital marketing services, rather than playing on potential clients' fears about their current underperforming strategies, you could highlight the successes of past clients. Statements like: "Join other thriving small business owners who have doubled their online engagement" focus on positive outcomes and real results, encouraging clients through aspiration rather than fear.

Respecting a client's autonomy is another critical aspect of ethical persuasion, and offering choices that allow clients to make decisions at their own pace is key. For services like specialised online courses, providing a free introductory lesson or a downloadable summary before requiring payment gives potential clients the chance to fully evaluate the offering. This approach not only respects their autonomy but demonstrates your confidence in the value of your service, thereby enhancing trust.

Finally, encouraging dialogue is fundamental in building a community around your brand. Simple strategies like inviting comments on social media posts or hosting Q&A threads can significantly deepen engagement. For example, ending a newsletter with an open question such as: "What challenges are you facing in your small business that you'd like help with?" and providing a direct link to schedule a consultation call can transform standard content into an interactive dialogue. These interactions do more than disseminate information; they invite active participation, making potential clients feel valued and heard.

Linguistic techniques for deeper engagement

Building on the ethical framework we've established, let's take a closer look at the specific linguistic and structural techniques of copywriting that enable us to effectively bridge the gap between what consumers think they want and what they actually need. By finding the perfect balance between the power of emotional appeals, logical arguments and the strategic presentation of product or service features, we aim not just to connect but to convert with integrity.

In copywriting as a small business owner, every word and sentence structure is an opportunity to engage deeply with potential clients. Emotional appeals are particularly potent as they tap into the visceral responses that can drive both the awareness of needs and the decision to fulfil them. For instance, consider an online financial advisor writing copy aimed at young families. Rather than just listing services like budget planning and investment advice, the advisor might evoke emotions through narratives that resonate with parental instincts, such as securing a child's future or building a family legacy. Here, the emotional appeal to protect and nurture one's family can motivate action more effectively than a straightforward listing of financial services.

Logical arguments also play a critical role in persuasive copywriting, particularly when they are used to illuminate the practicality of a service. For small business owners offering online consulting services, it's crucial to articulate not only the emotional gains but the logical benefits. Copy that explains how specific advice or strategies have historically led to revenue growth or reduced operational costs offers a compelling logical appeal. By demonstrating the clear cause and effect of utilising their services, these business owners can effectively persuade potential clients who need to see tangible outcomes before making a commitment.

Furthermore, the strategic presentation of features as solutions to deeper needs is a critical technique. This involves transforming features of a product or service into benefits that fulfil underlying needs. Take, for example, a software company that develops project management tools. Instead of simply listing features like task automation or integration capabilities, the copy should emphasise how these features free up time, reduce stress and increase productivity, directly addressing the common pain points of ideal clients. This approach shifts the narrative from what the product is to what it does for the client, making it easier for them to see the software as a necessary tool for enhancing their operational efficiency.

To ensure these techniques resonate authentically, it's essential to maintain a narrative that feels like a natural extension of a conversation, rather than it just feeling like a sales pitch. This can be achieved by integrating storytelling elements that weave through the practical applications of the services offered. For instance, sharing success stories of past clients or testimonials that align with the reader's aspirations can serve as powerful endorsements of the service's value, making the content not only engaging but relatable.

As we continue to explore these copywriting techniques, remember that our goal here is not just to inform but to transform. By writing content that speaks to both the wants and the deeper needs of our audience, we reinforce the connection between our brand and our clients. This approach doesn't just lead to better sales outcomes; it builds trust and loyalty, cementing our reputation as a brand that understands and cares for its clients.

Copywriting strategies for deeper connection and conversion

In the digital marketplace, interactive content is not just an option but a vital strategy for small business owners who wish to convert passive browsers into active participants and loyal clients. For those offering services online, the challenge isn't just to capture attention but to engage deeply and convert that engagement into sales.

Interactive content transcends conventional marketing by inviting the audience into a dynamic, participatory narrative. This isn't just about reading or watching; it is about experiencing. Advanced tools allow for the creation of personalised journeys that make each user feel uniquely seen and understood. For example, consider the potential of interactive quizzes tailored to deliver insights reflecting the user's specific responses. This personal touch not only captivates but guides them towards tailored outcomes and solutions, effectively showcasing how your services can meet their precise needs.

Visualise a personal coaching business that integrates an interactive assessment tool on its website. This tool could embark a visitor on a journey, beginning with questions about their professional aspirations and obstacles. As they progress, their answers could unveil customised content such as relevant case studies, enthusiastic testimonials and specific services that resonate with their goals. This strategic presentation does more than demonstrate the coach's capability; it positions their services as indispensable solutions.

Such interactive strategies excel in their dual ability to engage and inform, subtly nurturing the client's understanding of the service's value. They transform every interaction into an opportunity, gently leading the potential client towards a real connection with the benefits and making the decision to engage feel like their own. Incorporating live elements like webinars or workshops adds authenticity and immediacy, allowing business owners to solve real-time queries, showcase their expertise and directly interact with a captivated audience.

Imagine a digital marketing consultant hosting a live session on innovative social media strategies. This event wouldn't just share valuable insights; it would vividly demonstrate the consultant's expertise in real-time. Engaging directly with the audience in this live setting not only creates a strong sense of community but effectively highlights the consultant's depth of knowledge and approachable personality.

During these interactive sessions, incorporating clear and compelling calls to action is crucial. Offering special deals to attendees or guiding them to sign-up pages during the webinar leverages the peak of their engagement, facilitating instant conversions. Each element of the session, from content to delivery, is designed to enhance the perceived value of the services, making the decision to engage feel like an obvious next step.

To further captivate and retain the audience's interest, integrating gamification can transform the educational process into an exciting and engaging experience. Employing game mechanics like earning points for participating in discussions or unlocking badges for completing tasks not only makes the interaction fun but deepens the user's investment in the content. Such strategies enhance the enjoyment of the learning experience, significantly boosting engagement and increasing the likelihood of converting casual visitors into committed clients.

As we conclude this chapter, it's evident that interactive strategies are indispensable for effectively engaging and converting today's discerning online audiences. By moving beyond traditional marketing approaches and embracing the creation of meaningful, participative experiences, small business owners can forge deeper connections. These dynamic content strategies do more than fulfil immediate marketing objectives; they build lasting relationships and create a sense of trust, setting the stage for ongoing client engagement and loyalty.

Through these innovative engagement methods, small businesses are not just selling a service; they are inviting their audience into a transformative experience. This approach doesn't just capture attention; it turns everyday interactions into powerful moments of connection and conversion. It is here in the art of persuasive, participatory content that small businesses can truly take advantage of the power of their narrative, ensuring that every piece of content they produce does more than inform; it inspires, persuades and profoundly impacts their audience. This is the essence of fearless marketing and sales: a bold, transformative approach that makes every word count and every interaction meaningful.

Bridging the narrative: from insight to influence

As we wrap up our exploration in desire and deliverance, it's evident that the journey through marketing and sales is as much about deep understanding as it is about strategic communication. Our endeavour to align what clients think they want with what they truly need has revealed the profound responsibilities we hold as marketers: to guide, educate and, sometimes, gently reshape perceptions.

By delving into the roots of consumer desires, we've uncovered the complex variety of motivations that drive purchasing behaviours, from the allure of status and the quest for comfort, to the deeper yearnings for health and wellbeing. This knowledge empowers us to write copy and content that resonates deeply, blending emotional appeal with practical insights, thus transforming sales and transactions into meaningful, truly impactful interactions.

Our commitment to educational engagement and ethical persuasion forms the cornerstone of our strategy, ensuring that our influence is not only effective but respected. Through meticulously crafted copy that educates as it entices, we've demonstrated how to elevate the standard of marketing discourse, making every interaction an opportunity for growth and understanding.

As we transition from the strategies discussed in this chapter to the forthcoming exploration of selling the intangible in the next chapter, the lessons learned here lay a solid foundation. Selling services, especially those that cannot be seen or touched, requires an even deeper connection with potential clients – one that transcends the tangible to engage with their aspirations and deepest needs.

In the upcoming chapter, we will look at the nuances of marketing the services that lack physical form but hold immense potential to transform lives. We will explore how the principles of transparency, informed consent and the strategic use of emotional and logical appeals can be uniquely tailored to highlight the intrinsic value of intangible offerings. From personal coaching services to digital consulting, the challenge lies in making the intangible not only relatable, but indispensable.

The strategies we will uncover aim to refine our approach, ensuring that every piece of content does more than inform; it inspires and leads to deeper client engagement. This approach not only builds trust and loyalty but positions our brands as thought leaders who understand the complex interplay between consumer desires and their more profound needs.

8
Selling the Intangible and Making the Invisible Irresistible

In the world of service-based businesses, understanding the spectrum of tangibility is crucial. Services like graphic design, copywriting or weight loss coaching often produce visible, tangible outcomes: a new brand logo, a compelling article or a quantifiable reduction in weight. These results can be showcased, making it easier for potential clients to understand and appreciate the value being offered. On the other hand, services such as life coaching, spiritual counselling or psychic guidance deal primarily in the intangible. Their impacts – though profound – are not immediately visible, and their benefits can be abstract, such as increased self-awareness, peace of mind or clarity about life decisions.

Marketing intangible services requires a different approach compared to their tangible counterparts.

When a service's outcomes aren't immediately observable or quantifiable, your copywriting must bridge the gap between the abstract nature of the service and the concrete needs and desires of potential clients. This task demands a deep dive into the emotional and psychological benefits of the service, transforming abstract concepts into relatable, compelling narratives that resonate deeply with the audience.

For service-based business owners, particularly those operating online, the absence of physical evidence makes it imperative to employ copywriting that not only describes but vividly illustrates the transformative journey of the service. It is about painting a picture so clear and compelling that potential clients can envision the impact on their lives despite never seeing the service itself.

The key to effective marketing when it comes to selling the intangible is to engage deeply with the fears, aspirations and core needs of your audience. This engagement goes beyond simply listing service features or benefits; it requires telling stories that connect on an emotional level, showing prospective clients not just what they will gain but how they will feel during and after the transformation.

For instance, when marketing a life coaching service, the focus should not merely be on the process (sessions, techniques and so on) but on the journey of personal transformation. The narrative might explore themes of overcoming personal obstacles, discovering life's purpose or achieving a sense of balance and fulfilment.

Each element of the service should be linked to a clear, relatable outcome: a story that unfolds in the client's mind, illustrating the path from their current state to where they aspire to be.

To market intangible services effectively, embracing a fearless and bold approach is essential. This means being unafraid to talk about the emotional and sometimes vulnerable aspects of the service experience. Your copy should confidently address the common fears and hesitations that potential clients might have about engaging with something they can't see or touch. It should reassure them of the process, celebrate the journey and highlight the life-changing outcomes they can expect.

In doing so, your marketing material should not shy away from showcasing the depth and impact of your work. Whether it's through detailed client testimonials, vivid descriptive narratives or powerful case studies, each piece of content should reinforce the tangible benefits of your intangible service, making the unseen impossible to ignore.

Mastering the art of marketing intangible services is not just an advantage; it is a necessity. In an online marketplace flooded with options, standing out requires more than just listing what you offer; it demands creating an emotional connection that speaks directly to the heart of your potential clients. It is about painting such a vivid picture of transformation that they can feel the impact of your services, even if they can't see or touch them.

In this chapter, we'll look at the nuances of selling the unseen, unravelling the mystery of how to turn intangible benefits into compelling, must-have experiences. We will start by exploring the psychological principles behind why people buy intangible services and how to tap into these motivations with powerful storytelling. You will learn how to craft narratives that resonate, using emotional and sensory language to make abstract concepts tangible.

Next, we'll dissect examples of successful intangible service marketing, providing you with actionable insights and strategies. Whether it's life coaching, spiritual guidance or any service where the results are felt rather than seen, you'll discover how to highlight the profound impact of your work through case studies and testimonials that breathe life into your promises.

We will also cover practical techniques for creating a distinct and memorable brand voice that builds trust and a sense of familiarity and loyalty among your audience. You will understand how to leverage the power of personal branding to amplify your message and make your intangible services impossible to ignore.

Finally, we'll address the boldness required to market these services fearlessly. You will learn how to confront and overcome the inherent challenges, turning potential obstacles into opportunities to showcase the unique value you bring. By the end of this chapter, you'll be equipped with the tools and confidence to transform your intangible offerings into clear, compelling narratives that captivate and convert.

The psychological lure of the intangible

The essence of selling intangible services lies in understanding and utilising the psychological underpinnings that drive consumer decisions. People don't simply purchase services; they buy into transformations, experiences and the emotional outcomes these services promise. This chapter will explore the complex interplay of emotions and psychology that compels individuals to invest in services that lack tangible evidence, guiding you through the art of crafting narratives that not only resonate deeply but compel action.

At the heart of our exploration are the psychological principles that underpin consumer behaviour, particularly the emotional drivers that make intangible services appealing. As we've already discussed, consumers are often driven by an intrinsic desire for personal transformation, whether it's achieving peace of mind, enhancing self-confidence or finding purpose. These desires are deeply rooted in emotional needs and aspirations, making them powerful levers for persuasive copywriting.

To tap into these motivations, we must first understand the basic psychological needs as outlined by theories such as Maslow's hierarchy of needs or the psychological theory of self-determination. These frameworks suggest that beyond the basic needs for survival, these desires often manifest as a longing for transformation, aspirations for personal achievement and the need to alleviate various forms of pain. Additionally, there is a profound yearning for belonging, a universal drive that ties deeply into why individuals seek out certain services.

Transformation is a key theme for many who engage with services like life coaching or spiritual guidance. They may be driven by a desire to change their lifestyle, find new direction in life or enhance their mental health. For a marketer, the challenge lies in vividly illustrating how these services act as catalysts for such profound changes. Storytelling becomes an essential tool here. It involves narrating the transformative journeys of past clients, detailing the personal growth and profound changes they have experienced. This approach not only showcases the potential impact of the service but makes the abstract concept of transformation tangible and within reach.

Moving from transformation to aspiration, many clients are drawn to intangible services because they are chasing dreams that feel just out of reach. They might seek career coaching not just for guidance, but to catapult themselves into a dream role that seems unattainable. Here, the copywriting must do more than list service features; it needs to paint a vivid picture of future success. It should evoke the deep sense of pride, satisfaction and soaring confidence that comes from achieving these lofty goals. This narrative style helps potential clients visualise their success and emotionally invest in the journey towards achieving it.

Alleviation of pain is another compelling reason clients gravitate towards services like counselling or stress management. Whether the pain is emotional, psychological or spiritual, the promise of relief is a powerful draw. Effective marketing narratives will speak directly to the discomforts clients are facing and paint a hopeful picture of life beyond that pain. Sensory language can play a critical role here, describing not just the process of alleviation but the actual feelings of relief, peace and freedom. This makes the service not just a pathway to pain relief but a gateway to a new, liberated life experience.

Lastly, the need for belonging is a deeply ingrained emotional driver that can be particularly impactful when marketing intangible services. Many seek these services not just for personal benefit, but to feel part of a community or network. Whether it's a yoga class that connects like-minded individuals or a business coaching group that creates a sense of professional community, emphasising this aspect can be crucial. Marketing copy should highlight how services fulfil this need, creating a sense of inclusion and connectivity, thus offering more than just individual benefits. The copy provides access to a community that shares similar goals and values. By weaving these elements into a narrative, marketers can effectively bridge the gap between the intangible nature of their services and the tangible desires of their clients. The goal is to create a compelling, emotive and persuasive narrative that not only informs potential clients about the service but deeply resonates with their emotional and psychological needs, encouraging them to take the step from interest to action.

To solidify the understanding and appeal of your intangible services, talking about real-life examples and actionable insights within your narratives is essential. This approach not only adds credibility but brings your promises to life, allowing potential clients to envision the profound impact your services can have. Let's explore how to do this through client testimonials and descriptive case studies.

Imagine a life coach named Sarah who has helped numerous clients navigate significant personal transformations. Instead of merely stating that clients were satisfied with her services, Sarah talks in deep detail about their stories, providing a rich, end-to-end example of their experiences. For instance, she might share the journey of Leanne, a client who felt lost and directionless before starting the coaching sessions.

Before working with Sarah, Leanne was overwhelmed by indecision and self-doubt, waking up every morning dreading the day ahead. The narrative would describe Leanne's initial struggles vividly, painting a picture of her daily anxieties and the toll it took on her mental health. During the coaching process, Sarah's guidance helped Leanne uncover her core values and aspirations. She began setting achievable goals, slowly building confidence and clarity. The story would highlight key moments of breakthrough - perhaps the first time Leanne confidently made a decision without second-guessing herself, or the sense of empowerment she felt after completing a major goal.

As the narrative progresses to the 'after' phase, Sarah would describe the transformation in Leanne's life in sensory and emotional terms. Leanne now wakes up with purpose, feeling a deep sense of fulfilment and joy in her daily activities. She navigates challenges with resilience, and her relationships have blossomed due to her newfound confidence. This testimonial goes beyond a simple endorsement; it offers a detailed, relatable journey that prospective clients can see themselves embarking on.

In another example, consider a spiritual counsellor who specialises in helping individuals find peace and clarity in their lives. Instead of just claiming effectiveness, the counsellor could develop detailed case studies to illustrate the profound changes clients experience. One case study might follow Mark, who came to the counsellor seeking relief from chronic anxiety and a sense of disconnection from his life's purpose.

The case study would begin by detailing Mark's initial state: his constant worry, sleepless nights and feelings of isolation. Through a series of sessions, the counsellor used techniques like guided meditation, reflective exercises and spiritual discussions to help Mark reconnect with his inner self. The narrative would describe Mark's gradual journey from scepticism to a growing sense of peace and understanding. Key milestones, such as the first time Mark experienced a deep, meditative calm or his realisation during a session that led to a significant shift in his perspective, would be highlighted.

By the end of the case study, the counsellor would vividly describe the 'after' phase: Mark's life post-transformation. He now faces each day with a calm mind, sleeps peacefully and feels a profound connection to his purpose. His relationships have improved, and he approaches life's challenges with a newfound resilience and clarity. This detailed account transforms the abstract benefits of spiritual counselling into a tangible, relatable story that potential clients can connect with.

By incorporating such detailed and emotive client testimonials and case studies into your marketing, you bridge the gap between the intangible nature of your services and the concrete needs and desires of your audience. These stories not only demonstrate the effectiveness of your services but resonate on a deeply personal level, making the potential for transformation both believable and desirable. This narrative approach ultimately helps potential clients envision their own journeys of change, which guides them closer and closer towards choosing your services.

Using emotional triggers and pain points in your marketing

As we continue discussing the complexities of marketing intangible services, understanding how to effectively utilise emotional triggers and address pain points becomes crucial. This process isn't just about identifying what makes your potential clients tick; it is about weaving these insights into your narratives boldly and fearlessly, ensuring your message not only reaches but profoundly resonates with your audience.

The power of emotional triggers in marketing cannot be overstated. These triggers are deeply rooted in the human psyche, driving desires and decisions often on a subconscious level. For service providers, tapping into these triggers involves a detailed mapping of the emotional landscape your clients navigate and crafting your message to echo these emotions vividly.

For instance, let's consider a service like personal life coaching, which often deals with clients facing crossroads in their careers or personal lives. The emotional triggers here might include the fear of remaining stuck, the aspiration to achieve more and the excitement of new beginnings. A life coach needs to craft stories that not only acknowledge these feelings but depict a journey where these emotions are addressed and transformed. A narrative might describe a client who, feeling paralysed by fear of the unknown, embarks on a coaching journey that helps them embrace uncertainty and turn it into a stepping stone for growth. Here, the coach's role is depicted as a catalyst in turning fear into empowerment, making the intangible nature of the coaching process both relatable and desirable.

Addressing pain points goes beyond just standard problem-solving; it involves empathising with the client's situation and presenting your service as the solution to not just alleviate discomfort but transform it into a positive force. This approach requires a fearless acknowledgement of the client's struggles, using them as the fulcrum for demonstrating the transformative power of your service.

For example, consider a professional organiser offering virtual organising sessions. Clients might not initially see the need for such a service, thinking their disorganisation is manageable. However, by highlighting pain points such as wasted time searching for items, the stress of living in a cluttered space and the embarrassment of an unprofessional home office background during video calls, the organiser can illustrate a pressing need for their services. The narrative can follow a client from feeling overwhelmed and embarrassed to experiencing relief and pride in their new functional space, which the organiser helped create.

By describing specific, relatable scenarios such as the client hosting a successful virtual meeting without worrying about their background or questionable Zoom filters, the service is no longer intangible. It becomes a necessary solution that offers peace of mind and increased productivity. This not only makes the service tangible but crafts an emotional arc from distress to satisfaction that potential clients can envision for themselves.

The question of the ethics behind using pain points and emotional triggers

Using emotional triggers and addressing pain points in marketing often stirs a debate about ethics. Some might argue that it exploits vulnerabilities, but when done ethically and fearlessly, this approach actually enhances the connection between brands and consumers by demonstrating deep understanding and empathy. It is not about exploiting fears, but about acknowledging real issues and offering genuine solutions. This method is ubiquitous in advertising, employed by globally renowned brands to create resonant and successful campaigns.

Addressing pain points becomes a matter of ethical marketing when businesses use this strategy to genuinely help consumers solve problems rather than manipulating emotions for profit. For example, consider Nike's campaigns that often tap into the pain points of overcoming personal limits and the societal pressures in sports. Nike uses these triggers to not just sell athletic wear but inspire resilience and determination, connecting on an emotional level with anyone striving to 'Just Do It': overcome their hurdles and achieve their personal best.

Similarly, Apple frequently addresses the pain of outdated or inefficient technology in their marketing. By emphasising innovation, user-friendly design and cutting-edge features, Apple's campaigns resonate with consumers' frustrations with slower, less intuitive tech products. They present their products not merely as gadgets, but as essential tools for enhancing productivity and creativity, thus tapping into the pain points of modern life's demands.

Coca-Cola's advertising frequently evokes feelings of happiness and togetherness, associating the brand with joyous family gatherings and moments of celebration. Their 'Share a Coke' campaign, which personalised bottles with people's names, played on the emotional trigger of belonging and community, encouraging consumers to share the experience with loved ones. Another example is Dove's 'Real Beauty' campaign, which taps into the pain points of societal beauty standards and self-esteem issues. By showcasing people of various genders, races, shapes, abilities, sizes and ages, Dove addresses the emotional pain points related to body image and self-worth. This approach not only humanises the brand but deepens the emotional connection with consumers who feel seen and valued for who they truly are.

Being fearless in marketing means having the courage to really go deep into the real issues that potential clients face and showing them that you understand and can help. This involves more than acknowledging these pains; it involves demonstrating empathy and a commitment to solving them. For instance, when marketing a stress management workshop, the focus should shift from simply listing the features of the workshop to sharing transformative stories that resonate with the audience's experiences. You might describe the journey of a past participant – let's call her Emily – who struggled with severe anxiety during public speaking engagements. By participating in your workshop, Emily learned effective coping strategies and mindfulness techniques, which transformed her from someone crippled by anxiety into a confident speaker, admired by her colleagues for her poise and clarity.

This story does more than just outline the benefits of the workshop; it paints a vivid picture of Emily's transformation. It allows potential clients to visualise themselves achieving similar success, moving from a state of distress to one of control and confidence. By connecting the workshop's offerings to a real-life scenario, the narrative not only demonstrates the practical application of the service but emotionally engages the audience, making the intangible benefits of stress management feel tangible and attainable.

Using emotional triggers and pain points effectively also means being transparent about the journey. It is about setting realistic expectations and not shying away from the hard work involved in achieving such transformations. Emotional triggers are powerful tools in marketing because they tap into fundamental human experiences and feelings. When used correctly, they can turn abstract services into compelling, must-have experiences.

Turning insight into impact for fearless marketing

Throughout this chapter, we have looked at the complex yet crucial art of selling the intangible, exploring how to make the invisible not only visible, but irresistibly compelling. We have uncovered that the essence of marketing intangible services lies not merely in describing what they are but in vividly illustrating their profound impact on the lives of those who experience them. We discussed the importance of tapping into emotional triggers and addressing pain points with sensitivity and ethical mindfulness, transforming potential vulnerabilities into strengths that resonate deeply with your audience.

As we transition from the nuances of marketing intangible services, we venture into another area that is equally abstract and often shrouded in self-doubt: the belief in one's ability to write compellingly. Many service providers struggle with the misconception that they are not 'natural' writers, which can hinder their ability to market effectively. However, the next chapter will explore how this belief can be transformed. It will demonstrate that writing powerfully and persuasively is not a talent bestowed upon a chosen few, but a skill that can be honed and mastered through dedication, understanding and, most importantly, fearlessness.

In the upcoming chapter, I'm going to break down the barriers that hold many back from embracing their inner storyteller with strategies and insights that empower you to convey the essence of your services with confidence and clarity. By embracing the principles of fearless writing, you can write copy and content that not only informs and persuades but inspires and transforms. This journey will challenge you to push beyond your perceived limitations, encouraging you to explore the depths of your creativity and connect with your audience in ways you never thought possible.

As you move forward, remember that the ability to write well, like any other skill, grows from a blend of knowledge, practice and intrinsic motivation. By finding and working on the belief in your capabilities and understanding the impact of your words, you'll unlock the power to influence perceptions, shift paradigms and lead your audience towards meaningful action. This is where true fearlessness in marketing begins not just in the stories you tell, but in the very act of telling them. Let us now turn the page to a chapter that will not only refine your writing skills but redefine your understanding of what it means to be a writer in the world of marketing.

9

Finding Your Inner Wordsmith and Writing with Conviction

The notion that great writers are born with a pen in hand is a myth that weighs heavily on many, especially those stepping into the daunting world of online business. I know this feeling all too well. Having felt silenced for much of my life, the act of writing initially seemed like a reaffirmation of my fears rather than an expression of my voice. This perception of writing as a gift reserved for the chosen few can be particularly stifling for small business owners, for whom every word can tip the scale of success.

Let's dismantle this misconception right here, right now. Writing is a craft, much like any other aspect of entrepreneurship. It is not about inherent genius but about practice, resilience and the right mindset. My own transformation from a hesitant scribbler to a confident communicator didn't spring from unearthing some hidden talent; rather, it grew from my determination to find and express my identity through words, a journey from silence to a narrative that reshaped not only my business but my personal life.

The reality is reassuring: every one of us can develop effective writing skills. In the context of service-based business, where personal connection and authenticity reign, your unique perspective is not just valuable; it is vital. Writing well doesn't hinge on elusive natural talent but on the ability to figure out your authentic voice and convey it compellingly. This is fantastic news. It means writing effective copy is within reach for anyone willing to engage deeply with the process.

This chapter is dedicated to transforming how you perceive and approach writing from a source of anxiety to a powerful tool for connection and expression. We will shift from viewing writing as an arduous task to embracing it as a vital expression of your brand's identity and values. We'll explore practical methods to enhance your writing abilities, from grasping fundamental techniques to mastering a tone that resonates uniquely with your audience. Whether you're composing an email, updating website content or penning a captivating blog post, remember, writing is a skill akin to any other in business: it can be refined and mastered.

Understanding your unique voice

Every writer, every entrepreneur, in fact every human being carries a unique voice: an intricate melding of tone, style and perspective that distinguishes their words and brands from others. Recognising and refining this voice is crucial not just for clarity and coherence, but for authentically connecting with your audience. Your voice is your business's fingerprint on the world. It is how you tell your story, share your values and express your distinct approach.

As small business owners, particularly in the service sector, the journey to find and refine our own writing voice is not just a step towards better communication; it is a path to discovering our true identity within the business world. This voice is more than just a tool for writing; it is the very essence of how we connect with our audience, share our values and differentiate ourselves in a crowded marketplace. It is the heartbeat of our brand narrative.

To help you understand your unique voice, consider integrating some practical exercises into your routine:

1. Start with freewriting

Freewriting is your secret weapon in the battle against the perfectionism that plagues so many of us. Picture yourself: timer set, screen or notepad blank, a world of thoughts just waiting to spill out without the shackles of grammar rules or fear of judgement. This isn't just about filling pages but tapping into the raw nerve of your creativity. As you let the words flow unchecked, you bypass that nagging internal editor, the one that usually pauses your hand and questions every word. What surfaces during these sessions are your purest thoughts, unsculptured and unrefined, revealing patterns and ideas that structured thinking often masks.

This practice isn't just a writing exercise but a release valve for the pressures that typically accompany written tasks. Imagine lifting the weight of grammatical precision and perfect coherence from your shoulders. Suddenly, writing transforms from a daunting task into a liberating experience. It becomes a playground for your thoughts, where the stakes are non-existent and the possibilities infinite. This freedom not only makes writing more enjoyable but nurtures a writing voice that's authentically yours – perhaps unpolished, but incredibly real.

Moreover, when your mind wanders without borders, it's amazing what it can unearth. Freewriting is all about exploring the unexplored corners of your mind where fresh ideas and unique perspectives lie hidden. As you write, you might stumble across a brilliant insight into your business, or perhaps the seed of an idea that could grow into your next big project. This unstructured exploration allows your brain to make unexpected connections, the kind that are often stifled by the more rigid frameworks of day-to-day business thinking. It is in these freewheeling moments that true innovation can spark, offering you a glimpse into new directions or enhancements for your services that could truly set you apart in the marketplace.

Embracing freewriting is also about being fearless. It is about daring to meet your raw, unedited self and the myriad of ideas that reside within you without flinching or judging. This can be particularly empowering for business owners who often find themselves constrained by industry norms and client expectations. Here, in the privacy of your writing space, you can challenge those norms and play with ideas that you might have dismissed as too bold or unconventional for your business.

As you integrate freewriting into your routine, consider it a form of professional bravery: a way to fortify your creative muscles and discover your voice in its most natural state. This isn't just about getting better at writing; it is about better understanding who you are as a thinker, a creator and an entrepreneur. By making freewriting a regular practice, you're not only honing your writing skills; you are cultivating a fearless approach to expression that can transform all aspects of your business communications.

2. Writing a letter to a friend

Writing a letter to a friend is another transformative exercise that can help you find your natural writing voice: a tool of immeasurable value for any business owner. Imagine sitting down to write about your latest service or product, but instead of trying to come up with a typical marketing pitch, you're explaining it to a close friend. This approach strips away the formalities and pressures of business writing, allowing you to communicate in a way that's wholly genuine and deeply personal.

Consider how you would share your excitement about your new offering. You wouldn't just list features and benefits; you would express what makes it special to you and why you think it would matter to your friend. You would likely use a warm, conversational tone, filled with enthusiasm and sincerity. This style of writing - informal, heartfelt and direct - is incredibly effective because it mirrors the way you naturally express yourself when you feel safe and understood. It is not just writing but communicating with authenticity and passion.

This exercise serves multiple purposes. First, it helps you break down the barriers that often exist between 'business' communication and 'personal' communication. By writing to a friend, you're reminded that at the heart of all effective communication is the connection between human beings, whether they're friends, clients or potential clients. You learn to infuse your professional writing with the same authenticity and warmth that you'd use in a personal letter, making your business communications more engaging and relatable.

Secondly, it encourages you to articulate the value of your services in a way that's clear and compelling, free from jargon or overly technical language. This can be particularly enlightening for service-based businesses, where the benefits can sometimes feel abstract or intangible. Describing your service to a friend forces you to focus on the real-world impact and the emotional appeal, not just the technical features. You might find yourself explaining how your service can make life easier, bring joy or solve a particular problem – concepts that resonate on a human level.

Lastly, this task can dramatically enhance how you connect with your audience. By practising this way of writing, you'll find it easier to come up with your marketing material, social media posts or client communications that feel like they're coming from a real person, not a faceless business. This personal touch can be the difference between a potential client feeling sold to versus feeling seen and understood.

Incorporating this practice into your writing routine allows you to develop a voice that's not just professional but profoundly human. It shows that behind your business are real people with genuine enthusiasm for their offerings. This authenticity can help build trust and loyalty with your audience, turning casual followers into committed clients who feel a personal connection to your brand. So grab a pen or open a new document and start writing that letter!

3. Exploring different perspectives

Exploring different perspectives in writing is a transformative exercise for any business owner, especially those in service industries, where empathy and a deep understanding of diverse viewpoints are critical. When you engage in this practice, you select a notable event or challenge that your business has encountered and scrutinise it through multiple lenses. The exercise begins with you detailing the event from your own perspective, focusing on your personal reactions, thoughts and decisions. Next, you attempt to step into the shoes of a client affected by the same event, trying to capture their experiences and emotions. Lastly, you adopt the role of an impartial observer, offering a broad, analytical look at the circumstances.

This layered approach is beneficial for several reasons. It enhances your grasp of business challenges by allowing you to see them from various angles, which can lead to more profound insights into not only the events themselves but their broader implications on all stakeholders involved. This is particularly useful in understanding how clients perceive and react to your business decisions, which can aid in refining your services to better align with their expectations.

Moreover, adopting different perspectives can reveal new aspects of your own writing voice that may resonate with various audiences. Writing from your personal viewpoint often brings a natural authority and authenticity infused with your unique experiences and insights. When you shift to your clients' perspective, your tone might soften, becoming more empathetic and attuned to their concerns. Writing as an observer, your style could become more analytical, offering a balanced, detached critique of the situation.

This exercise also sharpens your ability to tailor your communication to different audiences. Regular practice in shifting perspectives helps you become skilled at modifying your writing style and tone to effectively connect with various groups, from clients and partners to broader public audiences. This flexibility is invaluable across many aspects of business, particularly in marketing and customer service, where understanding and addressing different viewpoints can dramatically enhance engagement and satisfaction.

Consider, for instance, you own a digital marketing agency that recently overhauled its project management software. This change, intended to streamline operations, initially led to confusion and frustration among your team and clients.

Start by writing from your own point of view. Discuss your decision to implement the new software, focusing on your anticipation of enhanced efficiency and the challenges you faced during its rollout. This perspective might highlight your commitment to improving service delivery, even when faced with unexpected hurdles. You could express your thought process, the challenges of integrating new technology and your proactive steps to address the teething problems.

Next, shift to your clients' perspectives. They might have experienced confusion or frustration with the new interface, leading to dissatisfaction or service disruption. Here, your writing should empathise with these challenges, reflecting on the clients' potential discomfort and the importance of clear communication during such transitions. This could lead you to consider the emotional impact of change on your clients and the need for supportive guidance when introducing new systems.

Finally, writing from an observer's perspective allows you to evaluate the situation more broadly. Discuss the general challenges businesses face when adopting new technologies, including the resistance to change and the learning curve associated with new systems. This detached view helps you critique both the decision-making process and its execution, possibly leading to insights about industry standards for implementing new technology and how your approach could be improved in the future.

By tackling this event from multiple viewpoints, you not only develop a more nuanced understanding of how different stakeholders perceive and are impacted by changes within your business, but you enhance your ability to communicate these complexities effectively. This practice cultivates a versatile writing style that can adapt to various narrative needs, ensuring that your business communications are not only comprehensive but deeply engaging.

This method does more than refine your writing skills; it fundamentally enriches your approach to business communication, making it more inclusive and reflective of the diverse experiences of those your business serves. Engaging in this practice regularly can transform your writing from a simple transfer of information to a robust tool for connection and understanding, crucial for any leader in today's multifaceted business environment.

The three exercises above aren't just tasks; they are invitations to explore and embrace your unique writing style. They challenge you to engage deeply with your thoughts and how you express them, transforming your approach to writing from a routine business activity into a powerful form of self-expression.

As we move forward, remember that refining your voice is an ongoing process. It evolves as you do, influenced by your experiences, your interactions and your growing business. The key is to stay authentic, allowing your voice to resonate with both clarity and emotion, thus forging a deeper connection with your audience. This connection is what transforms standard service transactions into meaningful, lasting relationships. By mastering your unique voice, you position yourself not just as a service provider but as a trusted partner – an ally – in your clients' journeys.

Building confidence by overcoming your barriers

Writing is an integral part of running a business, yet it's often fraught with personal anxieties and fears. Many small business owners, whether seasoned or newcomers to the online world, grapple with the fear of criticism or the nagging doubt that they're just not good enough to write compellingly. During my own journey, the transition from hesitancy to confidence in writing was deeply influenced by my past: feeling unheard and overlooked. I have learned that the key to overcoming this isn't finding a hidden talent but developing a clear, authentic voice through practice and persistence. As we've already discussed – and I hope you now understand – writing is not exclusive to 'natural-born writers'; it is a craft that can be honed with dedication, much like any business skill.

The first step in overcoming these writing barriers is to confront them head-on. Acknowledge that fear of criticism often stems from our own insecurities about our abilities. By recognising this, we can begin to separate constructive feedback from personal criticism, using it to fuel our growth rather than hinder our progress. To build your writing competence and confidence, I recommend engaging in regular writing exercises such as the ones outlined in the previous section of this chapter. These can take various forms, and when you start to feel more confident, you can move into things like daily journaling or weekly blogging. The key is consistency and purpose. Set aside a few minutes each day to write about something that matters to your business or personal growth. It doesn't have to be perfect; it just needs to be honest and authentic.

Experimentation is another crucial strategy. Try your hand at different writing styles and formats. If you're used to writing formal business proposals, switch to a more conversational blog style or even creative storytelling. This not only helps build your writing muscles but enhances your flexibility in communicating across different platforms and audiences.

One of the most empowering shifts in mindset I've experienced is learning to embrace mistakes as part of the learning process. Every error provides insight into how to improve. Instead of fearing them, view each typo, each awkward phrase, as a clue to better writing. This approach not only reduces anxiety but encourages a more playful, experimental attitude towards writing tasks. Moreover, overcoming writing barriers opens new doors for personal branding and career opportunities. Effective writing can further solidify your brand, showcasing your expertise and passion. It transforms your website, social media and marketing materials into powerful tools that communicate not just what you offer, but who you are.

Diving into writing, especially about personal or business challenges, can be daunting. Yet, embracing this with a fearless attitude not only enhances your skills but deepens your connection with your audience. Here are several prompts designed to ease you into writing confidently, addressing your fears head-on and showcasing the value you offer through your unique voice:

1. Today's triumphs

Begin by chronicling today's triumph, no matter how big or small. Whether it's positive client feedback or a new idea that sprang to life, write about what it took to reach this success and the emotions that came with it. This exercise isn't just about celebrating victories; it is about recognising the patterns of success in your daily life, which builds confidence and a positive mindset.

2. Current conundrum

Open up about a pressing challenge you're facing in your business. Describe the situation in detail, including how it makes you feel and the hurdles you perceive. Then, shift gears within your writing to brainstorm possible solutions. This prompt helps in two ways: it serves as a catharsis for your frustrations and morphs your mindset from problem-focused to solution-oriented.

3. Letter to future me

Imagine yourself one year from today. Write a letter to your future self, offering advice, encouragement and reflections on the current state of your business. What do you hope to accomplish by then? What fears do you wish to conquer? This exercise boosts forward-thinking and personal growth, encouraging you to envision a future where you've surpassed today's limitations.

4. Impact narrative

Reflect upon the distinct value your service offers. Write about a time when your service profoundly impacted a client. Describe the before and after, emphasising how your intervention brought about change. This prompt is powerful. It not only reaffirms the value you bring to the table but strengthens your conviction in your service's impact, which is essential when communicating with potential clients.

5. Dream dialogue

Create a fictional conversation between you and an ideal client who's hesitant to commit. Through your writing, address their concerns, illustrate the benefits of your service and guide them towards making a decision. This exercise sharpens your persuasive communication skills and builds empathy, allowing you to better connect with real clients' needs and objections.

6. Creative vision

Write a short piece of narrative that embodies the spirit of your business. Perhaps it's a day in the life of someone who's used your service or a narrative that captures the core message of your brand. This more creative approach allows you to explore and express your business's impact in a new, emotionally engaging way.

Each of these prompts is designed to push the boundaries of your comfort zone and encourage a fearless approach to writing. By regularly engaging with these exercises, you transform writing from a feared chore into a vital tool for personal and business growth. When embraced with open arms, these prompts will help you not only refine your skills but become more resilient in facing the challenges of entrepreneurship.

As we wrap up this exploration into finding your inner wordsmith and writing with conviction, let's recall the essence of what it means to be fearless, a theme we first touched upon in chapter one. Fearlessness is not the absence of fear, but rather the mastery of it. It is about recognising the tremors of uncertainty and using them as a springboard to leap forward into action rather than allowing them to paralyse us.

In this chapter, we've tackled some of the most common barriers that prevent small business owners from embracing their full potential as writers. We have discussed strategies to overcome fears such as the dread of criticism or the nagging doubt of not being 'good enough'. We have engaged in exercises designed to build your writing competence and confidence, encouraging you to experiment with different forms of writing.

These exercises are stepping stones to a more profound mastery of your voice and your message. Each word you write diminishes the fear of the blank page and the anxiety of what others might think, transforming them into opportunities for growth and connection.

Remember, good writing does more than convey information; it connects, persuades and resonates. It enhances your personal brand and opens new career opportunities by establishing you as a thoughtful leader and reliable expert in your field. Each paragraph you craft is an extension of your identity and an invitation to your audience to understand the world from your perspective.

As we move forward, embrace mistakes as inevitable milestones along the journey of improvement. Let each piece of feedback, whether positive or negative, refine and hone your approach. Continue to write with the knowledge that your unique perspective is invaluable, your words have the power to influence and your voice can leave a lasting impact on your audience. Because it really can!

10
Staying True to You

In the crazy world of entrepreneurship, the pressure to conform can be overwhelming. Business owners, especially those navigating the highly visible world of online business, often find themselves bombarded with advice on what success should look like. The allure of mimicking competitors who have seemingly cracked the code to prosperity is strong. Everywhere you look, there are blueprints, formulas, gurus and experts insisting that their way is *the* path to guaranteed success. This flood of conformity pressures entrepreneurs to fit a mould that may not align with their vision or values.

Yet, it's in this noisy marketplace that maintaining a unique voice and approach not only sets you apart but is essential to your business's authenticity and long-term success. Authenticity isn't just another marketing buzzword - not to me, anyway. It is the cornerstone of a brand that resonates deeply with its target audience. It is about being true to who you are as a business owner and how your business reflects your personal beliefs and passions.

For small business owners, the challenge doesn't stop at recognising the importance of authenticity; it extends to actively preserving it in the face of industry trends that constantly threaten to homogenise unique brands. Your unique voice isn't just valuable; it is critical. It is what attracts and retains clients who share your values and vision. When everyone zigs, your decision to zag – not out of contrariness but out of a commitment to your authentic self – can make all the difference.

Standing firm in your identity and values despite the pressures to conform is not only a rebellious act in today's competitive market but a strategic one that can lead to more meaningful connections with your clients and sustainable success for your business. Embracing your authenticity is not just about being different, but about being true to your core. This truth resonates with your audience, creating a loyal community that believes in what you stand for as much as they believe in your products or services.

As we wrap up *Fearless Words: How to Write Impactful Copy for Authentic Influence and Sales*, let's explore a few more strategies for identifying and nurturing your unique business voice, ensuring that it consistently reflects across all aspects of your business from your marketing materials to customer service interactions, and even the way you handle internal operations. You will learn how to conduct a 'voice audit' to ensure your brand's communication is aligned with your authentic self, and how to resist the temptation to echo the industry giants if their path doesn't align with your vision.

Additionally, we'll examine case studies of businesses that have thrived by sticking to their authentic selves in the face of generic industry norms. These stories will highlight not just the moral satisfaction of authenticity but its practical, profitable impacts. By maintaining a genuine brand voice amidst a trend of conformity, these businesses have not only differentiated themselves in crowded markets but successfully built deep connections with their audience, leading to increased client loyalty and brand advocacy.

Moreover, this chapter will address the fear that often accompanies the decision to stand out rather than blend in - the fear of losing out, being judged or failing. We will discuss how to leverage this fear as a driving force behind innovation and client engagement. Instead of shying away from what makes you different, we'll talk about how to highlight these aspects boldly and fearlessly, turning potential vulnerabilities into your greatest strengths.

By the end of this chapter, and this book, you will be equipped with the tools to confidently claim and articulate your authenticity, transforming what makes you unique into your most powerful business asset. This isn't just about surviving in a competitive market; it is about thriving by being unabashedly yourself, securing a place in the industry not despite your differences, but because of them. In doing so, you will not only build a brand that is true to your values but inspire others to pursue success on their own terms, creating a ripple effect that promotes diversity and innovation across the business landscape.

The risks of conformity

Navigating the online marketplace often compels business owners to glance sideways, eyeing competitors and industry leaders and so-called gurus as benchmarks for success. This instinct, while rooted in the desire to survive and thrive, can lead businesses down a precarious path: the path of conformity. Emulating others may provide short-term gains or a semblance of security, but it often comes at a significant cost: the loss of your business's unique identity.

The primary risk of conformity is becoming invisible, which is a one-way ticket to destroying your personal brand. When businesses sacrifice their unique traits to adopt what seems popular or safe, they inadvertently erase the very qualities that could make them stand out. This not only dilutes the brand but can lead to a disconnect with the core audience that was originally drawn to the brand's unique offerings.

Moreover, businesses that continually shift their identity to mirror others are often seen as insincere or unreliable, and trust, once eroded, can be challenging to rebuild, especially in an online environment where interactions are already depersonalised. Consider the story of a once-thriving online coaching business that initially stood out for its bold approach to personal development. The founder's unique perspective and authentic voice resonated deeply with a dedicated client base. However, as the market landscape became more competitive, the pressure to keep up with top-performing rivals led to a gradual shift in their messaging and methods. This shift aimed to replicate the surface-level features of successful competitors, from their marketing tactics to their programme offerings, neglecting the deep, client-centred approach that had fuelled their original success.

Over time, the business noticed a decline in client engagement and retention. Long-time clients began to drift away, drawn instead to newer coaches who offered a more genuine and less derivative experience. The business's attempt to mimic competitors not only diluted its distinctiveness but made it less appealing to those who valued its originality.

Another example is a small boutique marketing firm known for its creative and unconventional campaigns. In the beginning, their fresh ideas and quirky approach landed them a series of successful projects and a loyal client base. However, as the firm grew, the pressure to compete with larger, more traditional agencies led them to adopt a more conservative and generic marketing style. This change was meant to attract a larger number of clients but instead caused them to lose the smaller, niche businesses that had been attracted to their original creativity. The firm not only lost clients but faced turnover within their creative team, who no longer felt aligned with the firm's new direction.

These examples highlight the dangers of straying too far from one's founding principles and the essence of what made the business special. For small business owners, particularly those operating online, the challenge is not just to resist the urge to conform but to find ways to amplify their unique voice in a market that often rewards conformity. This requires a keen understanding of what makes your business unique and a commitment to maintaining these qualities despite external pressures.

To maintain your unique business identity, it's crucial to regularly revisit and reaffirm your core values, USPs and mission. These should act as a compass for all business decisions, ensuring that even as you adapt and evolve, you remain true to the vision that set you apart from the beginning. Engaging in open dialogues with your client base can also provide insights into what they value most about your service, guiding you to build upon those aspects more fervently. Furthermore, leveraging the very platforms that may seem to encourage conformity - social media and online marketing - can actually be a way to highlight your uniqueness. Instead of using these platforms merely to broadcast, use them to engage in genuine conversations with your clients, share behind-the-scenes content that reflects your business's personality and create content that starts discussions rather than just adding to the noise. This approach not only reinforces your brand's identity but builds deeper connections with your clients, enhancing their loyalty and trust.

Innovating rather than imitating, and overcoming the fear of standing alone

Innovation doesn't always mean inventing something new; it often means presenting your existing services in a way that is fresh and deeply aligned with your brand's voice. This could involve packaging your services differently, highlighting lesser-known benefits or simply communicating your offerings in a way that better reflects your brand's unique perspective.

The digital landscape offers myriad tools and platforms for creativity and differentiation. From personalised email marketing campaigns to interactive webinars that showcase your expertise and personality, the opportunities to reinforce your unique identity are vast. Each interaction is a chance to remind your clients why they chose your business over others and to demonstrate that staying true to your brand is not just a marketing strategy, but a commitment to authenticity.

Walking your own path in business, especially one that diverges from the well-trodden routes of competitors or industry standards, can often feel like standing at the edge of a cliff. The fear of stepping into the unknown – facing potential rejection or witnessing your efforts culminate in failure – is visceral. It is a fear that tightens your chest, that keeps you up at night with endless 'what ifs'. This fear isn't just a nuisance but a profound challenge that tests your resolve and commitment to your unique vision.

Yet, there's a raw, undeniable power in creating your own lane and embracing that path. It is about understanding that every major decision comes with its risks but also its rewards. Standing alone doesn't have to mean standing isolated; it can mean standing out, being a shining light for others who share your vision but haven't yet found their voice. It is about building something that genuinely reflects who you are and what you believe in, not just what the market expects or what has been successful for others.

To navigate these fears and build resilience, start by acknowledging these emotions as a natural part of the entrepreneurial journey. Recognise that feeling scared doesn't mean you're doing something wrong; it often means you're doing something profoundly right, something really brave. Connect with other entrepreneurs who have carved their own paths. Their journeys, filled with both setbacks and successes, can offer not only comfort but practical strategies for resilience.

Do not forget that building confidence in your unique path involves a commitment to your vision. Regularly revisit the core reasons why you started your business. What were the values and passions that sparked your venture? Keeping these at the forefront of your mind can reinforce your resolve when doubts creep in. Moreover, setting small, achievable goals can help build momentum and reinforce the validity of your chosen path, showing that progress, no matter how incremental, is still progress.

Lastly, embrace your vulnerability as a strength. Because that's what it is. Sharing your fears and uncertainties doesn't make you weak; it makes you relatable. Real. Normal. It turns your journey into a story that others can see themselves in, and this creates a deep connection with your audience. They move from simply investing in a service to investing in a relationship with someone who isn't afraid to be real, to be human.

By really owning this authenticity and resilience, you not only overcome the fear of standing alone pave the way for a brand that resonates deeply with those it serves. Your courage to remain true to yourself becomes your business's most compelling narrative, inviting others to join you not out of mere necessity, but out of belief in what you stand for.

Authenticity isn't just a strategy

Embracing authenticity in your business is not just a tactic for standing out in the crowd; it is a strategic approach that leads to long-term benefits, building a foundation of trust and loyalty among your audience and clients - past, present, and future. When you consistently align your business practices with your true self, you not only attract the right kind of clients but cultivate deep, enduring relationships that extend beyond transactions. More than a strategy, the beauty of authenticity lies in its magnetic power to attract people who resonate with your values and vision. These are not just any clients; they are the right clients: those who appreciate what you uniquely offer and who are likely to remain loyal because they believe in the ethos behind your brand. This alignment is not something that can be forced or faked. It emerges naturally when you are true to your principles in every aspect of your business, from your marketing messages to the way you handle client interactions and even how you respond to challenges.

Loyal clients become more than people who pay you; they often turn into brand advocates: enthusiastic supporters who will champion your services to others. This word-of-mouth endorsement is invaluable as it comes with a level of credibility no amount of advertising can buy. Your authentic clients will share their positive experiences with their networks, which can lead to new clients who are already predisposed to trust you because of the testimonials they've heard from people they themselves trust.

Moreover, maintaining authenticity in your business practices can lead to sustainable growth. When you operate in a manner that is true to your values, decision-making becomes more straightforward and your business strategy becomes more focused. You avoid the pitfall of chasing every trend or mimicking competitors, which can dilute your brand and lead to strategic missteps. Instead, you invest your energy in initiatives that align with your brand's core, which not only enhances efficiency but ensures that your growth is sustainable and not at odds with your identity.

This authentic approach also provides a profound sense of fulfilment. Knowing that you are succeeding not by masquerading as something you are not but by being genuinely yourself brings a level of satisfaction that transcends financial success. It affirms that your unique qualities and viewpoints are valuable and that there's a place in the business world for your distinct brand of service. This realisation can be incredibly empowering and can fuel your passion and motivation to continue growing and evolving in ways that remain true to your founding principles.

Finally, remember this simple yet powerful truth: you can't say the wrong thing to the right person, and you will never be able to say the right thing to the wrong person. This maxim underscores the essence of authenticity. When you are true to yourself in your business, you naturally attract those who appreciate and seek what you offer. Conversely, those who do not align with your values or offerings are likely not the ideal clients for you, and no amount of manipulation disguised as marketing will create the meaningful connection you desire and deserve.

In embracing and advocating for your true self, you create a business environment where the right relationships flourish: those founded on mutual respect, shared values and genuine engagement. These relationships are not only more enjoyable but more likely to endure, providing a stable foundation for both personal satisfaction and business success.

As we close, consider authenticity not just as a strategy but as a guiding principle: one that informs every decision, interaction and innovation. By staying true to yourself, you build a business that not only survives but thrives, enriched by clients who believe in your mission and supported by practices that reflect your true identity.

Now, you have a choice

As we draw this journey to a close, let's circle back to where we began: the understanding that true fearlessness is a myth. It doesn't exist in the unattainable way we often imagine. It is not the absence of fear; it is the mastery of it. It is feeling the tremble and doing it anyway. It is hearing the voice of doubt and choosing to speak louder. This is your call to embrace every fear and every uncertainty as the first step towards the extraordinary.

Remember, your voice is more than just decibels; it has depth. It is your influence in the world, your unique echo in the cacophony of the marketplace. There are people out there who need to hear what you have to say, who are waiting for someone like you to stand up and articulate their thoughts, their fears, their dreams. Your words can be the north star for those lost in the noise, looking for direction or affirmation. Never underestimate the power of your voice. It can be the voice that leads a change, the voice that offers solace, the voice that sparks innovation.

Your opinions, your insights and your visions are worth sharing because they are inherently yours – unreplicated, genuine and resonant. The world doesn't *ever* benefit from you hiding your light. This is a fact! So shine boldly, even blindingly, into the corners where fear and conformity gather. Your brilliance can dispel the shadows that often shroud innovation and truth.

It starts with a choice: the decision to be fearless, even when your instincts urge you to contract. Decide to expand. Decide to occupy the space you've dreamed of. This isn't about ignoring fear but about transforming it into the fuel that propels you forward. Each moment of courage, each act of vulnerability is a step towards a more authentic and impactful existence.

You can find your voice and use it with a thunderous impact. You can carve out a path that is wholly yours. You can embrace your unique perspective and share it with the world that is far more ready for your authenticity than you might believe. It begins now, with a simple yet profound act of belief in yourself and your potential.

As you step forward from here, let each step be guided by the truest parts of yourself. Let your decisions be coloured by your authentic desires, not the expectations of others. Be daring in your ambitions and unwavering in your values. Let the essence of who you are be the touchstone of your business and your life.

The journey of entrepreneurship is as much about discovering yourself as it is about building a business. It is about peeling back the layers of who you think you should be to reveal who you truly are. It is about standing in that truth unapologetically and fearlessly.

As you move forward, remember that fearlessness is not a trait possessed by the few but a choice available to all.

Choose to be fearless. Choose to be heard. Choose to impact the world in the way only you can.

And so, with a spirit emboldened and a heart truly committed, step into your path of authentic expression. In each word you craft, in every service you offer and through every connection you make, know that you have the power to influence, inspire and lead. You possess everything necessary to not just compete but set a new standard.

You are more than capable; you are transformative. Let your voice echo boldly, let your ideas illuminate the dark and let your journey be unmistakably, unapologetically, fearlessly your own.

Afterword

I hope these pages have served not just as a guide but as a catalyst for your own fearless exploration into the world of impactful communication and authentic branding. Writing this book has been a journey of introspection and expression - painful at times, joyful at others - and always a reflection of my own continuous quest to speak with courage and live with authenticity.

Every chapter, every example and every strategy shared here has been steeped in the belief that our voices matter - profoundly so. Your voice is not just a tool for business; it is a conduit for change, a builder of communities and a creator of opportunities. The processes and practices discussed are more than methodologies; they are invitations to step into a space of vulnerability and strength, where true growth happens.

This book is a call to reject the silence that fear imposes and to embrace the boundless possibilities that fearless living offers. It is an encouragement to not only speak but do so boldly, to not only follow but lead with conviction, and to not only exist but thrive dynamically in your authenticity.

As you close this book, may you not see it as the end but as a beginning. The start of a more fearless chapter in both your life and your business. Remember, the world doesn't just need more noise (there's plenty of that!); it needs deeper, more meaningful voices.

It needs *your* voice.

Go ahead, write your first word, launch your idea, pitch your project and do it with the full force of your unique perspective. There are people out there waiting to hear exactly what you have to say. They are waiting for someone like you to lead the way, someone who embodies their values and speaks to their hopes.

Thank you for sharing this journey with me. May your path be brave, your words resonate and your brand shine brightly in a world that awaits your mark.

Dare to disrupt, dare to defy and, when they tell you to quieten down, speak louder.

Because the world doesn't just need voices like yours; it's damn well better with them.

Acknowledgements

A heartfelt thanks to my friends, family and loved ones (who know exactly who they are) for enduring my spectrum of emotional performances: moaning, ranting, raving, crying and a considerable amount of swearing, especially in those chaotic days of mid-June 2024 before this manuscript hit the proofreading table.

Your patience has been heroic.

To my clients from 2011 to now, thank you for giving me the stories, the challenges and the victories that have stitched this book together. Without your voices and your journeys, these pages would be hollow.

You have not only fuelled my writing but been the backbone of my confidence to share these words.

To the drag queens clad in feathers and glitter who strut their fabulousness on random Tuesday afternoons in Soho, thank you for inspiring me to just be... me.

You are living proof that there's no excuse not to shine in our own unique ways.

And to Fred. You forgave me for those missed meals when chapters consumed me more than your dinner time. Thank you for your (fleeting) patience and for not toppling my laptop off the desk in protest.

Your presence, the meows, however demanding, were comforting constants amidst the clattering of keys.

Lastly, a nod to the music that carried me through the highs and lows of writing. Your rhythms and lyrics were the pulse behind the words I typed and kept me sane.

(Mostly)

About the Author

Georgina L. Nestor is the founder of Fearless Words, where she channels her deep-seated love for words and stories into empowering business communications. She specialises in turning even modestly-sized online audiences into major sales figures through compelling copy that leads to five, multi-five, and six-figure launches for small business owners.

Georgina's journey into the world of words began as a young teen, when she first encountered hip-hop and became captivated by the genre's complex lyricism and the potent ability of words to connect, influence and transform. This early passion laid the foundation for her career in storytelling and persuasive communication.

Fresh out of the University of Kent with a BA (Hons) in English and American Literature, Georgina began her professional writing career in 2011, working part-time as the content manager for one of the UK's leading online music platforms. There, she wrote and edited blogs, reviews and interviews, becoming the voice behind many of the site's compelling stories while working full-time as a PA in investment banking.

In 2018, Georgina took a leap of faith and went full-time with her copywriting business, Fearless Words. She is dedicated to transforming ideas into engaging narratives that do more than inform - they inspire and drive results.

Why choose Fearless Words?

Georgina's approach combines her expertise in narrative structure with a profound understanding of consumer psychology to create messaging that resonates across diverse platforms while staying true to a brand's core values. She offers bespoke copywriting services, self-study courses and ebooks designed to enhance your brand's communication, impact and income.

Discover more about how Georgina can amplify your brand's voice at **www.fearlesswords.co.uk**.

Connect with her on Facebook, Instagram, and LinkedIn by searching "*Georgina L. Nestor*" to tap into a world where authenticity meets success.

Printed in Great Britain
by Amazon

54743233R00104